WOMEN
WHO
illuminate

WOMEN
WHO
illuminate

A COLLECTION OF ILLUMINATING
STORIES THAT WILL BRIGHTEN
YOUR HEART'S JOURNEY

kate butler
BOOKS

kate butler
B O O K S

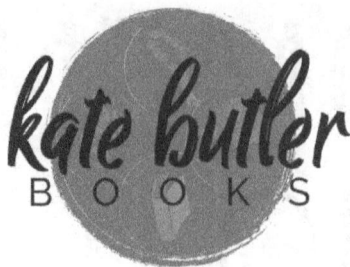

First Edition

Copyright © 2019 Kate Butler Books

www.katebutlerbooks.com

All rights reserved.

Design by Margaret Cogswell
margaretcogswell.com

This book is dedicated to those who use their brilliance to illuminate the world. We were all born with a unique brilliance that is waiting to shine, and then shine brighter. The world needs what you have and is waiting for your light to shine bright. So, thank you, brilliant you, who chooses to rise up and illuminate your brilliance. We honor you for all that you are and the ripple of light you will spread throughout the world.

enjoy the unfolding ...

FOREWORD: HOW TELLING MYSELF "YES" LED TO AN AWARD-WINNING DOCUMENTARY

Dr. Angela Sadler Williamson

Our journey is made of moments and they vary from small to large. When I reflect on my *My Life with Rosie* journey, I realize it was a lot of small moments that led me to the one large moment that changed my entire path.

I first met Rosa Parks in April 1998. Before I met her, my husband, who is also her cousin, and his aunts told me she attended all of her cousins' weddings and special events. But I really didn't believe it. And why would I? Not in my lifetime would I ever believe a civil rights legend would attend my bridal shower. As evidenced by the photos that are now in the United States Library of Congress, I was very wrong. Not only did she come, but she gave me one of my most treasured gifts, an autographed copy of her book entitled, "A Quiet Strength," welcoming me to the family. And she, the mother of the Civil Rights Movement, even played bridal shower games with me and my guests!

She came to our wedding, where the entire wedding party stopped and stared in awe. She was our most esteemed wedding guest. Later, I'd see the city of Detroit's love for Cousin Rosie when she passed away in 2005; the streets of Detroit were lined with thousands of people, including elementary school children. Even though I observed how one woman made a huge impact on society, it didn't occur to me to produce a documentary about her for another ten years.

In 2007, I left my job as a sales marketing producer at FOX 11 & FOX Sports West to pursue a doctoral degree and teach in higher education. In the fall of 2007, I started teaching as an adjunct professor at a small Christian university in Orange County, CA. Although I was initially teaching at several colleges and universities, eventually that small Christian university would be the only place I taught while I pursued my doctoral degree at Capella University.

During the next seven years, I completed my doctoral degree and applied for tenured positions at local colleges and universities. Unfortunately, I couldn't get a single interview despite completing over 200 applications, and, although I was offered Resident Faculty positions twice at the university where I was teaching at the time, the offers were revoked, and the positions were given to other instructors. After the second revocation, I left that university for a position as a Digital Marketing Manager at a mortgage company in Southern California. It would be a three-month disastrous decision which would end with me leaving the job and being unemployed. Then, in 2015, a tragic moment would start the journey that changed my life forever.

At the beginning of 2015, not only was I jobless with significant student loan payments, but, in March, my beloved father-in-law died unexpectedly. The emotional load I was carrying became too much and I started eating my way through my depression. Since I was jobless, with plenty of time on my hands, my husband asked me to plan his father's memorial service.

My father-in-law's estate was very organized and included a budget for his memorial service. The budget was enough to produce a short memorial video celebrating his life. I enlisted the help of former colleagues in the entertainment industry to complete the video and it received a lot of compliments from family and friends following the memorial service.

Little did I know that creating that memorial video would launch the trajectory that changed my life. During this time, my father-in-law's two sisters stayed with us. His younger sister, Carolyn, who was also the personal caretaker and attendant for our cousin Rosa Parks, stayed with us. During her stay, she would tell me stories about working with Cousin Rosie and the work she was doing to keep our cousin's legacy alive in the City of Detroit. She and her friends' efforts continued Cousin Rosie's passion for the community, and especially children.

Since Cousin Rosie's death in 2005, Aunt Carolyn received many commendations for this work, including an award from the City of Los Angeles. It was during my conversations with her that I first considered capturing our family's oral history and the idea of *My Life with Rosie* was born. However, it would take encouragement from good friends to give me the final push to start the project.

In May 2015, I started pre-production for my first documentary by reaching out to former colleagues to help with the production of the film. I also reached out to a Rosa Park's biographer, Dr. Jeanne Theoharis, who kindly agreed to provide insight to Cousin Rosie's life after the boycott. In October 2015, in 72 hours, we shot *My Life with Rosie* in New York, Detroit, and Canada.

My Life with Rosie would be in post-production for two years because everyone working on the film could only work on it part-time while working their "day jobs." I also joined the International Documentary Association and found a talented music composer in Ireland who would help me understand the process of creating original music for a feature film. Although we were working in the "cloud" and would never meet each other in person, she would become a dear friend through the process. Also, in the fall of 2016, I returned to the small Christian university in Orange County as an adjunct instructor and was invited to join the Writers Guild of America West.

I had two goals for the documentary: the first was to make sure our son had an artifact of his family's incredible legacy; the second goal was to, hopefully, gain a full-time university position teaching. As a result, the documentary was created with an emphasis toward secondary and higher education. It was edited with discussion questions after each segment of the movie so instructors could lead classroom discussions. However, Dr. Theoharis, who was so influential on the film's content, the music composer, and the editor had a different suggestion for *My Life with Rosie* – the film festival circuit. Each of them approached me separately about considering this option because they believed the film would be well received by festival directors. I had no idea this was an option because I had only known about large film festivals, but the music composer and editor told me that many of the smaller festivals would love our documentary.

When I agreed to try the film festival circuit, the music composer and editor both agreed that I would need to re-edit the documentary deleting the discussion questions; thus, creating a second version of the documentary, which we called the "film festival" version. In May 2017, we finally completed the documentary and I sent the documentary to Dr. Theoharis for review. She suggested two changes – one was a minor editing change, but the second was an extensive change and required me to contact officials in Detroit who didn't know me or anything about the film I was producing.

Therefore, I spent a summer trying to get in touch with several nonprofits in the Detroit area, without much luck. Dr. Theoharis is an award-winning author and I really wanted to incorporate her suggested changes, but I was faced with the decision to wait or move forward with the project. At that point, I was sitting on a finished documentary for five months without submitting to any film festivals. After careful consideration, I decided to submit *My Life with Rosie* to film festivals in November 2017. Three days after submitting it to several festivals, it was accepted into the Culver City Film Festival, and on December 10, 2017, *My Life with Rosie* premiered at a movie theater in Los Angeles. I saw a lot of great films, including documentaries, during the festival and I was in awe of being accepted into my first film festival and seeing it in a movie theater.

The awards ceremony was the day after my movie premiere, so I didn't ask my family or friends to attend. It was a very long awards ceremony and it was getting to the end of the ceremony when the film festival director announced the "best of show." I was congratulating another filmmaker on her win when I heard someone call my name. The assistant for the film festival told me they just called my name and I needed to walk to the front to win my award for "Best Documentary" for the film festival. To say I was in complete shock would be an understatement, as I never expected to win "Best Documentary," and I was embarrassed that I missed my name being called.

This would be the part of the story where I wish I could say that *My Life with Rosie* immediately started screening in film festivals across the country, but it would take four more months, and rejections from four festivals, before it would screen again. During that time, I was featured in two magazines, but I didn't get any closer to my second goal of a job offer for a full-time teaching position. My journey wasn't following my desired path and I couldn't understand why that wasn't happening.

The filmmaker I was congratulating at the Culver City Film Festival when I missed hearing my name being called got in touch with me after the festival. When she learned I was a new filmmaker, she emailed me a list of film festivals to apply to and told me to use her name in my cover letter to the festival directors. After following her advice, *My Life with Rosie* started getting accepted into more festivals. As of today, the documentary has been in sixteen film festivals and won sixteen awards.

And yet, I was still adjunct teaching. I appeared in two more magazines for colleges and universities for whom I wasn't "good enough" to hire full-time. However, they couldn't pass up the opportunity to promote an adjunct instructor's successful documentary about national icon Rosa Parks. Even though I had a multi-award-winning documentary, I was an emotional wreck because I wasn't accomplishing one of my professional goals – teaching full-time at a university or college.

Somehow, the awards kept coming. I was contacted by the co-chair of the Belle Babb Mansfield Committee in August 2018. She read an article about me in the spring edition of the "P.E.O. Record" magazine. Every year the committee chooses a person who best exemplifies the legacy of Mansfield, the first woman to successfully pass the bar exam and practice law in the United States, and the co-chair believed that I would be an excellent candidate and wanted to know if I was willing to be nominated. I was highly motivated by any encouragement I could get, and I said I'd be honored to be considered. Before the end of August 2018, I was named the 2019 *Belle Babb Mansfield Award* recipient, which included screening my movie and giving a keynote speech on the campus of Iowa Wesleyan University in March 2019.

Before I went to Iowa Wesleyan University, I screened the documentary at Concordia University Irvine and Valdosta University during Black History month in 2019. At Valdosta University, I participated in a special panel entitled, "Protecting Your Family's Legacy," sponsored by the African-American Studies Department. The entire scope of my desire to be an educator would change and I wouldn't even realize it until after my visit to Iowa Wesleyan University. Although the documentary was getting a lot of attention, and as of December 1, 2018, was on Amazon Prime, I was still teaching as an adjunct to make the payments on my student loans.

As a *Belle Babb Mansfield Award* recipient, I participated in a student-led panel discussion. I was introduced to the student moderators, who had auditioned with many others for the opportunity to participate on the panel. One especially enthusiastic student moderator told me her participation was a highlight of her college career. Although I had been meeting students like the student at Iowa Wesleyan University, it wasn't until my conversation with her that I realized I was limiting my professional scope on educating college students. Even though I hired a college student to design the graphics package for *My Life with Rosie*, I was still focusing on my traditional teaching experience. I thought I could only make a difference to students if I was lecturing in a university setting; however, I realized my greatest impact came from taking the time to share my journey creating *My Life with Rosie* and introducing a new side of Rosa Parks to a wide range of students.

The student's comment allowed me to replay the moments of my amazing journey to bring this story to a mass audience and I began to wonder if maybe my entire professional goal wasn't aligned with my life's purpose. However, I didn't have time to really reflect about it because I still had to deliver a keynote address and receive my award. In my keynote address entitled, "150 Years of Women Changing America's Story," Iowa Wesleyan University's website described me "as a woman being a new voice for a historical movement." I thanked the university for the compliment, but I wanted to impress upon them that I was just a "vessel" given an extraordinary opportunity to continue to change America's story that was long ago changed by women who challenged the "*status quo*" of their day like my cousin Rosa Parks and Belle Babb Mansfield.

Those women didn't let hearing the word "no" distract them from achieving their life's mission. I realized my ten years of hearing the word "no" finally led me to say "yes" to myself when I started writing *My Life with Rosie*. It took me over ten years to fully grasp the big picture of my professional journey as an educator and realize that it cannot be limited to one class or one college or university, but my impact should be more far-reaching if I wanted to impact young people's lives.

Receiving the *Belle Babb Mansfield Award* was never on my professional or personal life plan, but it took that experience to help me realize that I was, in fact, fulfilling my heart's desire. After the ceremony a lovely woman came up to me and told me how much I encouraged her, and she gave me a card and a book entitled, "Women Who Impact." She told me to read the note when I was back home. Denise McCormick's note encouraged me by telling me that my story should be in her publisher's next book, "Women Who Illuminate," and she would help me make that happen. She even quoted my advice when she presented the opportunity to me by writing, "as you shared this morning [in the student-led panel discussion], the worst I can hear is 'no'." I couldn't say "no" to a person sharing my own advice.

Our life's many moments are designed to help us change our thinking as we fulfill our goals. In my case, I had to change my thinking and climb out of the emotional pit that I dug for myself. When I did, I created a tribute to one of America's most beloved heroines that will forever change how she is viewed by national and international audiences.

ABOUT DR. ANGELA SADLER WILLIAMSON

Angela Sadler Williamson, Ph.D., is an independent filmmaker, speaker, and adjunct instructor in the Communication Studies Department at Concordia University Irvine. A former producer and copywriter for the Orange County NewsChannel, Fox 11 Television, Fox Sports West, and Prime Ticket, Dr. Williamson has over twenty-five years of experience in the broadcast television, cable advertising, healthcare, financial, municipal government, and higher education industries. A multiple Telly awards recipient, Dr. Williamson has a doctorate in Human Services with a specialization in Management of Nonprofit Agencies from Capella University in Minnesota. She is also the 2019 recipient of the *Belle Babb Mansfield Award* and has been featured in *Women Who Rock with Success* and *Black Girls Allowed* magazines, and *Civil Women* on PBS. Dr. Williamson is currently a member of P.E.O. Sisterhood serving as the Publicity Chairperson for the Inland Empire and the Writers Guild of America West. In December 2018, she released her award-winning documentary about her cousin, Rosa Parks, *My Life with Rosie*, on Amazon Prime. To contact Dr. Williamson, go to www.drangelasadlerwilliamson.com.

table of contents

xvi

xvii

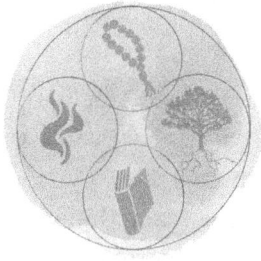

INTRODUCTION

Kate Butler

I was scheduled to attend a conference three hours away. About a year earlier I had found myself struggling with postpartum depression. Of course, I was not aware of this at the time. It was not something anyone was really talking about. I did not know the signs, what to look for, or know anyone else who felt the way I did. I just thought I wasn't quite as good at this "mom thing" as everyone else around me who made it look so seamless. In my world, the primary thoughts that were swirling around were those of overwhelm, stress, and sadness. I was not unhappy with my husband or children, that was the strange part. I did not have any big reason to feel these feelings, but I still felt them. This made me feel even more guilty since I did not have a good reason and I kept trying to convince myself that I should be happy. Which, of course, made things even worse. It was a vicious circle, that went on in the parameters of only my own mind, in silence, by myself. No one knew the struggle I was in except for me. It was a lonely and depressing place to be.

As a result, things in my life began to show the effects. I was not motivated in my work and our finances were suffering. I was not happy within my self, so my husband and I were not connecting the way either us wanted to. My relationships in general were challenged. I was not

1

happy with myself, so how could I be happy with other people? The answer was, I couldn't. I began to see some of the main areas of my life deteriorate … my job, my finances, my relationships, and my health. And then I heard someone say something that changed everything. "At some point, you have to consider that it can't be everyone else. At some point, you may need to look at the common denominator in all of this, and that may just be you."

They were absolutely right. It couldn't be everyone else's fault all of the time. I needed to take some serious personal responsibility and realize that if I was the one with all the problems, then I must be playing a part in it. I just did not know how.

By simply being open to taking responsibility and being open to how I could change, things began to appear in my life. This was the beginning of my pathway to miracles, although I did not know it at the time. But it certainly was a miracle how soon after having this realization a friend invited me to attend a personal development retreat. This was something that had never even been on my radar before. But after attending, was life changing.

I not only learned how to take full personal responsibility, but I also learned how I was allowing, creating, or promoting everything that was in my life. I realized everything that was present in my life was a result of what I was thinking about a year ago. So, if I wanted to change what my life looked like in the future, then I needed to change my thoughts today. I did just this, and it was, again, miraculous how the circumstances in my life began to drastically change too. I can remember sitting at the kitchen table with my husband discussing how we wanted to send our daughter to a private preschool because we thought she could use more of a challenge that the school she was already attending. When we looked up the tuition for the school, we experienced serious sticker shock. We weren't sure how we would pull it off. I told my husband I was going to apply the techniques I had learned and that I was not sure how it would work out, but that I was sure that it would. We had a deadline for the application. So without knowing how we would pay for it, we signed on the dotted line and committed to attend the school. Each day I visualized paying the tuition with ease and grace. I would imagine our daughter excelling and flourishing in the environment. I would connect with the feeling of gratitude for experiencing such an amazing year at this school. Five days later I received a call from a former business associate. She said she was working on a project and they were looking for a contractor to help them for a few months. She then shared what the compensation would be and the pay was for the exact same amount of money that we had to pay for tuition. It was exact down to the dollar. I was shocked, yet not in disbelief. I did believe this would happen. I did not expect it so quickly or down to the dollar, and I did not know how, but I did believe it would come. And so it did. There were many, many other things like this that began to unfold in every area of my life. Having this evidence consistently show up allowed me to trust my intuition and tap into even more. I began following this internal guidance.

This set me on a path of wanting to learn more about personal development. My motivation was coming back, and I began to have a desire to truly live the life I was meant for. I believed there was more for me to do.

About a week before I was scheduled to attend this personal development conference, I began to receive these feelings that I should not attend. The feelings became so strong one day that I called my husband at work to tell him. This was a very rare occurrence; since my husband is an engineer and works on classified information, he can rarely take calls at work. But this felt urgent and I was able to reach him. I shared with him my feelings and he responded with support by saying, "You are probably just worried about leaving the kids. Don't worry, I will take good care of them and they will be fine. It's only for the weekend." This made sense and I thought he was probably right. So, I brushed it off.

The next day my dear friend was over visiting, and we were talking about the upcoming weekend. As we began discussing this conference, she said to me that I seemed apprehensive about going. I shared my conversation with my husband with her. She related that, with our children being so young, it might be hard to leave them, but she also agreed they would be fine.

I knew in my heart of hearts this wasn't it, that there was more. But I ignored that inner guidance and shrugged it off.

Two days later I was packing for the trip and was almost ready. I was wearing a casual black dress, the perfect ensemble to be comfy for the ride and also be ready to network and mingle as soon as I arrived.

I was packed, dressed, and ready. The last thing I needed to do was put deodorant on. As I went to do this for the millionth time in my life, the deodorant stick somehow fell out of my hand all the way down my dress and left behind a thick, long white line across my black dress. I had never, in all my years of wearing deodorant, ever had this happen. I couldn't believe it. Something inside me told me that things were just not right. But I was in a rush to get on the road, so I ignored it.

Once I was in the car, I had forgotten my sunglasses, so had to jump out and run back in the house. Then I forgot my tickets to the event, so ran back inside again. Then I was finally ready to leave. I looked down to buckle up and my necklace was broken. It felt so strange. Something was just off. But I convinced myself that I was just in a rush, and once I got on the road and settled into the drive everything would be fine.

As I began my drive, I started playing a Brené Brown book on Audible, which I would normally eat up with a spoon. But this drive was different. A little over an hour into the drive I realized I had not actually heard one word of the audiobook that was playing. I was in my own world that entire time, but I could not tell you one thing I was actually thinking about. It was like I was somewhere else.

I decided I needed to reset and that I would stop to get some coffee or tea. I took the next exit and got off the highway. I did not see any coffee places, but there was a Chick-fil-A where I could get an iced tea.

That was perfect. The shopping center it was located in was new. So, I thought it was odd that there appeared to be construction. When I pulled into the parking lot of Chick-fil-A I was met with a big sign, "CAUTION." Then the next sign I read was "STOP." Then next sign was "PROCEED WITH CAUTION." This was so strange. There was actually no work being done, yet these signs were here, and it felt like in that moment they were placed there just for me. I was shaken to my core. I put my car in park in the middle of the drive-through, closed my eyes, lowered my forehead to the steering wheel and said a prayer. I called my angels in and asked them to protect me. I was already now in the process of traveling, so I asked my angels to please protect me on the rest of my travel and to keep me safe. I opened my eyes, put my car in drive, and got my iced tea. As I left, there was another sign that said, "Warning." It sent chills down my spine. This was a feeling too strong to ignore. I realized I had ignored all the warning signs before, but now, I was ready to listen. Once again I asked my angels to surround and protect me, and I began driving.

I was back on the highway for less than ten minutes when a man plowed his car into the back of my car at the speed of eighty miles-per-hour. I was in the left-hand lane. When I felt the crash, my immediate reaction was to steer onto the shoulder of the highway so I did not crash into the car in front of me. Once I steered onto the shoulder I had very little control and my car began hitting the guard rail. I looked out of my window and saw that on the other side of the guard rail was a straight drop down. I just kept praying that I would not flip over and crash down the hill. I said out loud, "No. This is not my time. This is not it. I need to be here for my family. I need to be here for my girls. This is not my time." And within a few moments I came to a stop.

All my airbags were deployed. My car was completely totaled. The driver was distracted, causing him not to see me, and he received five citations at the scene of the accident.

I walked away without a scratch.

I truly believe this was an exit point in my life, having experienced other exit points before. But I was not ready to go. This was not it for me.

I learned two things in that moment.

I first learned that your intuition is never wrong. It will never guide you off your path. Your intuition always knows what is for your highest and best, even if it doesn't make any logical sense at that time. Your inner guidance comes as a gentle whisper, a quick thought, a strong feeling, or sometimes through physical evidence like signs. But it is available to guide you on the right path at all times if we are just aware enough to listen.

In that sharp moment on the edge in between worlds, I also learned that there was still a lot of light left in me to shine in this world. It became clear that I was born with a light inside that shines differently than anyone else—and so were you. We all were.

Our only purpose in this world is to shine that light as brightly as possible so that each person's unique brilliance illuminates the world in the way that only they can.

You are here to illuminate. Shine brightly, my friend.

ABOUT KATE BUTLER

Kate Butler is a #1 Best Selling Author, Certified Professional Success Coach and International Speaker. Kate has been featured on HBO, in the Huffington Post and many other televisions, news, and radio platforms.

Kate's children's books, More Than Mud and More Than Magic, have received the prestigious Mom's Choice Award for Excellence®, the Readers Favorite International Book Award® and have also been endorsed by popular children's brands, Kidorable® and the Garden State Discovery Museum™.

Kate received her degree in Mass Communication and Interpersonal Communication Studies from Towson University, MD. After 10 years in the corporate industry, Kate decided it was time to fulfill her true passion. Kate then went onto to study business at Wharton School of Business at The University of Pennsylvania and received her certificate in Entrepreneur Acceleration.

Kate now follows her soulful mission to guide people to activate their core brilliance so they can impact people's lives and ignite their own. In pursuit of this mission, Kate has impacted thousands of lives through her books, keynote speeches, live events, and coaching programs in her business as a Certified Professional Success Coach.

Ways to work with Kate:

Coaching - From 1:1 Coaching to Online Group Coaching, Kate offers a programs that facilitate guaranteed success in both your personal and professional life.

Publish a Book - If you have always dreamed of sharing your story or publishing a book, then let's connect and discuss how we can make this happen for you! We take care of all the logistical work, so you can just enjoy the writing process! You are guaranteed to become a Best-Selling

Author in Kate's Publishing Programs.

Speaking - Whether you are hosting an intimate women's circle or a massive seminar, Kate would love to support your work by speaking at your next event. Kate is not just an inspirational speaker, but also an experiential speaker, bringing the audience through exercises that will create energy shifts and mindset expansion right there on the spot. The audience will leave feeling inspired, empowered, uplifted and with a renewed sense of clarity. Kate's main mission is to inspire women to align with their soul's path and she would love to partner with you in order to impact more people!

Author Visits - Inspiring children is where it all begins, and Kate does this through her school visits. Kate travels around the world to share her books with schools, often times with her daughter, Bella, who co-wrote More Than Magic. Through reading their books and sharing the writing and publishing process, they encourage children to believe in themselves and their dreams.

To connect with Kate or to learn more about her work, we welcome you to visit www.katebutlerbooks.com.

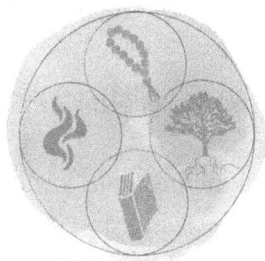

THE DARK SIDE OF AMBITION

Gina Fresquez

"Whoa! Are you ok?" This was the exact comment my concerned husband said as he walked in on me in our bedroom curled up with the dog, sobbing on the bed. It was a Saturday in fall 2012, the first full day I had off in a long time since I was working a demanding corporate sales career with tons of travel AND building my coaching and consulting business on the side. To say I was "hustling" was an understatement. I was completely strung-out, stressed, and burned out. As my mother would say, I was "burning the candle at both ends," and we all know how well that turns out!

What was I crying about? Well, being the super ambitious person I have always been, I was really poor at giving myself permission to take a break. You see, on this day all I wanted to do, all I CRAVED to do, was to veg out on the bed with my pup, binging on movies to relax ... but instead I found myself dealing with a war within my head.

The ambitious part of me was saying that I had so much stuff to do and I should take advantage of this day. I should work on my business, I should email that prospect back, I should write that newsletter, I should invoice that client, I should research my next project, all-the-things; but another part of me was completely exhausted feeling like I needed a break to recuperate from such a long week, but I felt extremely guilty

9

taking a "lazy" day. The problem was my mind was having a tug-of-war on what to do.

All of my ambition was building up inside of me and I was so extremely hard on myself. I had so much judgement around what it looked like to become successful, partnered with the fear of failing, that I pushed for perfection and a perpetual state of busyness.

Enter my husband that day, and through my tears and snuffles, I exclaimed "I just don't know what to do! I want to stay in bed, but I have so much stuff to do!"

"So, relax. Why can't you just relax?" he asked.

GREAT QUESTION. And one that I could not answer because I felt so conflicted and stuck.

THE PLIGHT OF THE AMBITIOUS

Innately, I was a go-getter, super ambitious person who had big ideas and was always going after my dreams no matter what. This has been a gift in many ways, contributing to my achievements and success, but it is also part of the plight of the ambitious.

Why couldn't I just let it go, relax, or take the easy route? Why was I so dang hard on myself? Maybe I was afraid to show up fully, to make a wrong move or to screw up, afraid to disappoint someone. I never felt like it was enough or like I could keep up. And even having a super supportive, loving partner who just wants me to be happy, he still couldn't understand why I was so hard on myself, crying on the bed. This made me feel isolated, like something was wrong with me.

ENTER SELF DOUBT AND FEAR

Then I realized this situation was a completely self-inflicted problem. No one was pushing me but myself. No one was telling me what to do or how to be. I had stretched and stressed myself out to my own detriment, and my ambitious self was causing the war of self-doubt and fear inside.

I realized that the ambitious woman is never going to settle for the *status quo* and is determined to make the most out of her life. With that being said, part of the ambitious journey is constantly pushing ourselves to the edges of extreme change and growth, which are uncomfortable and cause these moments of self-doubt, fear, and indecisiveness.

These edges of expansion are bringing us into new levels of life—new missions, new passions, areas of growth, new awareness, and pivots. We are pushing our own boundaries, setting our sails for new and different experiences that allow us to improve and level up. Constantly changing and evolving, these experiences are present, and present often for the ambitious woman. On the outside it may look like she is strong, has a lot going for her, and can handle anything with stride, but I can promise you that may not always be how she feels about herself.

When you are ambitious, always working towards growth and self-improvement, you are constantly on these borders of change, and inevitably without a doubt, you come up against fear. It doesn't matter how evolved we are, it will happen and doesn't go away, as it is part of the process of constantly moving into a place you've never been before, a place of uncertainty.

ILLUMINATING FEAR

With that uncertainty comes fear. You see, fear will always be around to stop you, to protect you, to tell you what you cannot do, and to keep you in the same place because it was designed this way.

Fear comes from one of the oldest, most primal parts of your brain that is wired to keep you safe, an instinct. In the simplest form, for fear, change equals death. So, it will work extremely hard to keep you alive. Fear loves staying in the *status quo*, keeping you from the unknown and uncertainty. It feels safe there.

Now, this has served humankind for thousands of years. In the past, going out of the cave at night might get you eaten by the saber tooth tiger. So, your fear was built to stop and save you … but in our modern times, there is a shift in how we relate to our fears. We now have different kinds of fears, that only really show up in our minds, things that we worry about that are not life-threatening nor always grounded in reality, but still keep us stuck (or in my case, sobbing in my bed.)

"Getting clear on what you're scared of can instantly defuse ticking anxiety bombs." - Danielle LaPorte

Some fears are conscious, some are not. As an ambitious woman, you might not know you are experiencing fear because it is sneaky and many times shows up as perfectionism, procrastination, laziness, paralysis, avoidance, stress, anxiety, being too busy, or people pleasing. Bringing these things into the light with awareness will help us recognize and understand fear and self-doubt better. Which, in turn, will help us get out of our own way to achieve the success we crave on our journey.

CHANGING OUR RELATIONSHIP WITH FEAR

Now, there are many ways to approach fear. Some say you must bust through your fears, tell your fears to shove off, push them aside, or that you must have no fear.

But that is not the approach that I believe in or teach. I DON'T BELIEVE IN BEING FEARLESS. Fear is a part of you. We cannot cut it off and ignore it. I believe that fear is trying to tell us something and by listening to it for a moment, giving it some love and attention, letting it express itself and what it wants, and working through the discomfort and pain together—just like you would with any loving relationship—you can remove these blocks standing in your way. By bringing fear out of the shameful darkness and into the light, we can choose to work with it in a loving and gentle way, instead of fighting with the fear holding you back.

"If you try to get rid of fear and anger without knowing their meaning, they will grow stronger and return." – Deepak Chopra

ACHIEVING CLARITY

Inevitably, as part of this ambitious journey, when approaching an edge and entering into a space of change and uncertainty, we become unclear, doubting our next move or course of action. You start asking yourself, "Should I do this? Am I doing the right thing? Will I make a mistake? Why do I always need a push? I'm so different than everyone else. Why can't I just relax? Why can't I just be happy with the way things are?" As long as fear is taking over and in charge you will remain uncertain, unclear, and immobile. That is why it is so important to first address the fear before we can become unstuck and move forward.

Over the years I have developed a process of working through fear and self-doubt to help myself and my ambitious clients win the war within their heads and get out of their own way on their journey to success. By working through these steps of addressing fear, you will reach a point of clarity which will help you make confident decisions with more ease and take inspired action in moving forward. When you achieve this clarity, you can show up fully as yourself with solid confidence, leverage your strengths, and feel more momentum and less resistance in pursuing your goals—smooth sailing towards your goals.

FOCUS ON THE JOURNEY

But in true ambitious style, the cycle will repeat. Because we are never satisfied with the *status quo*, we are constantly evolving and pushing the edges into new territory over and over again. We can be so hard on ourselves, pushing, striving, and never giving up, so much so that we tend to focus on the destination or end game, sacrificing ourselves, our health, and our sanity in the process. One of my biggest learning has been to focus less on the destination and more on the journey. Knowing that things will always be changing and leveling up and there will always be uncertainty. Therefore, if I stay present, rely on my internal clarity compass by knowing how I want to feel every day and working with my fear to get to that next step, I can navigate this journey with more ease, confidence, and freedom.

THE IMPORTANCE OF CONNECTION

As I embrace my inner ambitious woman, I now know I am never done with evolving and pushing my limits. Therefore, it's important to know I am never done with working through my fears. They will pop up again, and I will go back and repeat the process. And while I am up for the challenge on my journey, many times it can feel isolating and like no one gets me. This is why the best thing you can do is connect with others who do get it. I have found that surrounding myself with other like-minded, ambitious women who are always going through the same rinse-and-repeat process of pushing the edges and evolving has been a game changer for me. Connection and ongoing support is so extremely valuable and is the cornerstone of what will help you continue to remain successful in this process. As ambitious women we can support each other in getting out of our own way and accelerate our success on this journey. In it together.

So where am I today? Well, the story of me crying in bed and the war within my head is one that I tell my clients often as a reminder of where I was and how far I've come. But I'm not going to lie, it's a constant practice to stay present, focus on the journey, and always be working through my self-doubt and fear as I pursue my ambitious goals. But I have so many more tools to use and a crew of women to support me on this journey. Richard Bach says it best, "You teach what you most need to learn." My goal is to constantly be teaching how to embrace this ambitious life by navigating change and the unknown and succeed with fear along for the ride.

ABOUT GINA FRESQUEZ

Gina Fresquez, MS, CHC, is an international speaker, best-selling author, and success and leadership coach for high-achieving, ambitious women entrepreneurs and leaders in male-dominated industries.

Gina holds a master's degree from the University of Arizona and coaching certifications from the Institute for Integrative Nutrition and HCI Transformational Coaching Method, as well as having experience in stress management, mindset work, and startup and small business consulting.

After spending many years in corporate technical sales and consulting, Gina's dream of becoming an entrepreneur came true in 2012, when she started her first side hustle. Since then, she has enjoyed her own ambitious journey of strategically and intuitively coaching her clients through overcoming overwhelm, removing fear and self-doubt, banishing burnout, increasing confidence, and making decisions with more confidence and ease. Gina currently accomplishes this through one-on-one coaching, group programs and workshops, masterminds, and her signature women's retreats.

Do you have a group of people who would be interested in Gina's message or enjoy having her speak or facilitate at a workshop or event? Send her a note at hello@ginafresquez.com.

Contact:
www.ginafresquez.com
Facebook: @GinaMFresquez
Instagram: @GinaMFresquez
LinkedIn: @gina-fresquez

Connect with your new tribe and join my supportive Facebook group, The Ambitious Journey with Gina: www.facebook.com/groups/theambitiousjourney

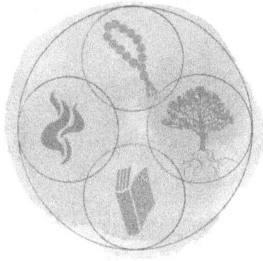

IN THE MOMENT, WE SHINE

Jennifer Granger

Hello Sunshine,

I have a surprise for you.

This chapter is all about YOU!!!

I am so grateful for our time together as you wrap up in the illumination from each of these pages. As you read each of these words, I am humbled that they are birthed into the world to bring a pure light to you.

You see, I'm just like you, Sunshine. I awaken each day to shine my light and then after the setting sun, I begin to rest my head as the darkness surrounds my pillow. We are really all the same, but oh so very unique in how our light shines in this world.

I am a passionate creator of stringing words together on a page so that they may offer a safe space to be present in that moment. Each moment is all we have, and my creative spirit soars when I can offer a way to help you, Sunshine, stand fully present in your moment and experience what it is meant to be, in that moment.

I discovered my peace in the moment, even in the most turbulent of times. I also have discovered that when I focus on gratitude for the experience of that moment, it opens an opportunity of infinite possibilities to move forward into the next moment, and the next, and the next. It's like a constant beating heart once you become present in the moment. The past no longer lingers and the future turns into a vision of possibility, not certainty.

You see, Sunshine, I've discovered that my soul's path is all about creating space for a journey of infinite possibilities. Doesn't that just simply sound divine? My journey to realizing this illumination of my soul's path has been quite an adventure because of one simple truth—love.

When you peel back all the layers of you, to get to the one singular truth of you, your heart can't help but speak to you. It's like the unfolding of a rose that seems infinite, but then it finally reaches its peak bloom. You breathe in the sweet scent of the rose and it's now gifted you with its truth—love.

Just like my heart space is filed in this moment right now as I speak directly to you … soul to soul … inner guide to inner guide. Sunshine, it is pure illumination when you are connected to your heart voice, because then you know you are living in your truth and have all the answers to all the questions. The heart voice speaks in truth and love only.

Let me show you what I mean by listening to your heart voice. This is why I said at the beginning that this chapter is all about you. I am on a mission to help you connect to your heart voice. Would you mind taking a little journey with me, Sunshine, so you can see what I mean by Creating the Space for a Journey of Infinite Possibilities?

Yes? Yes!!!

Before we get started, make sure you are comfortable and ready to settle into the journey.

Imagine yourself now walking along a beautiful beach. The sand between your toes and the sunlight in your hair relaxes you so much that you just simply begin to melt into the journey step-by-step. As you hear the ocean waves, you are reminded of the natural rhythms of our earth. The salt air feels comforting with each breath you take. The waves wash in and reach your toes in the sand and you feel a sense of release—the releasing of all the mind chatter from your head. The waves are now all you hear, and the ocean has taken away the mind chatter for a cleansing in the salt water. Mother earth is so very kind to take on this chatter and clear it out.

How are you feeling, Sunshine? As you surrender to the peace of this walk along the shore, you notice the birds dancing in the waves. Off in the distance of the ocean you can see dolphins breaking free for moments at a time to dance in the water. They are there just for you, Sunshine, because I am creating this space. Do you see how the simple string of words on this page have given you the moment to be? Yes, it's the gratitude I have for this gift that allows me to gift it to you, Sunshine.

When you came into this journey, you weren't quite sure where it was headed, but now you trust that it's safe. We are still on the beach and you're stopping now to pick up some seashells and beautiful bits of sea glass. The colors are glittering in the sunlight. You place a few in your pocket because you want to hold this memory.

As you reach down to rinse off the sand from your fingers, you notice a small raft coming toward you. The waves are much calmer now as the raft comes ashore. There is a small wooden box inside the raft. It's a simple carved box with an inlay of gold in the shape of a Sunshine. This is my gift to you Sunshine.

You reach down to take the box and you hold it now in your hands. The sun is reflecting so strongly on the golden inlay—it's illuminating the space you are standing in now, Sunshine. You can feel the warmth from its glow.

You are so curious what's inside, aren't you? Go ahead and take a peek inside, Sunshine. Imagine yourself opening the box to reveal the gift I have selected especially for you … the gift is YOUR journey of infinite possibilities. Close your eyes, Sunshine … what do you envision in your box of infinite possibilities?

You've created the space with me to be so very present in this moment with these words. And you now can come to this special place to be free from the mind chatter, free from the pressures and turbulence in the world. This is the sacred space I've created just for you, Sunshine.

Do you feel the infinite possibilities before you?

Do you feel the love I poured into this gift?

Do you hear that voice of truth and love speaking to you? That's your heart voice.

You can carry it with you just like the shells and sea glass in your pocket.

And I promise you one more gift, too. I promise you that you can even create your own space with all the magical sights, sounds, and experiences. It's really easy when you get very quiet inside and listen to your heart voice. And when you get to that space and you hear your heart voice, then you know you've reached your soul's path. There's no fear on this path, there is only a strong curious attention to taking the next step moment by moment. What you soon discover is that there are some other soul paths who are nearby you. They know you, Sunshine, because they too hear their heart voice. In fact, when you discover these kindred souls, they shower you with love and gratitude, and you so freely return all the love and gratitude as well.

How do you feel, Sunshine? Do you feel loved? Your heart voice will be there to tell you how much you are loved. It will fill you up with so much love that you can shine the beacon on others each day. Don't worry, Sunshine, this kind of love is completely infinite. It's not possible to run out of love when you spend time with your own love, on your soul's path.

So, you might be wondering how you can get this experience outside of these pages. Oh, and you might even feel a little unsure of how best to stay on your soul journey or fully hear your voice. Here's the most exciting gift about infinite possibilities. There really are so many ways to experience being fully present in your life moment by moment. I'm going to share a little Sunshine Miracles List with you. I would also share with you too that this isn't even the full list, because once you are on your soul's path there will be daily practices or rituals that you discover that are aligned to your sweet soul.

SUNSHINE MIRACLES LIST

Meditation

This is the superpower of the miracles list because when you are connected to your inner voice, that heart voice, you have all the answers to your questions. And, Sunshine, it's okay if you don't always act on the answers, because we are a soul in human form which is filled with imperfections and perfections all at the same time. I can promise you though that if you get quiet for at least five to ten minutes a day, you will be able to quickly get back to the space you created for your infinite possibilities. If you haven't tried meditation before, there are so many resources found with a little research. Trust me, Sunshine, the moment you decide to meditate every day, the universe will deliver all the resources and people to you in response to your commitment and action.

What's that, Sunshine? You want to start right now?

Okay, here's a few little quick tips to access the miracle of meditation:

1. Sit comfortably. You can choose to sit on a pillow, the floor, a comfy chair. Whatever works for you and your body.
2. Open the palms of your hands and rest them on your knees. Having your palms open is a signal to your inner guide that you are open to universal guidance or truth coming to you.
3. Now close your eyes and let your tongue come to a comfortable place on the roof of your mouth. You will feel your jaw relax.
4. Wiggle a little again to settle into your position.
5. Now take a deep inhale through your nose and let your lungs expand with the moment.
6. Now exhale again through your nose and feel your body settle into a position of comfort.
7. Repeat two more times (or as much as you need to release from your physical world.)

8. You then simply stay in this space with you and your heart voice. If you notice mind chatter or thoughts entering, that's okay. Just notice how they can also float away in balloons or clouds that you imagine. Stay in your meditation for as long as you feel is right. You can play some simple music if that helps you. I've also found a nice little water fountain to be a great tool to create my space for the mediation journey.
9. Once you are ready, you can bring your awareness back to present
10. Congrats! You are a meditation guru!

Visualization

I like to think of this miracle as the "story of me" in HD, because you are seeing your future through all of your five senses as if you are already living out your soul path or dream. So, to help you see how simple this can be, I wanted to share a silly example of how I future-vision my "movie star parking" when I head to a crowded location. As I'm driving there, I say to myself, "I am so happy and grateful I have movie star parking." And while entering the parking lot, I visualize an empty space between two white lines. I see it so clearly sometimes that I almost pull into it before I find it. That's how powerful my future-vision has become. See how that works?

Now let's take it up a notch and add the power of writing and visualizing. When you have very specific goals that you want to achieve by a certain date, it is so important to claim it in writing. Pick a date out into the future and write your story in HD. Where are you? What are you wearing? Are you alone or with anyone? What does your location look like? Is it warm, cold, really hot? Indoor or outside? What scents and environmental activities are surrounding you? What do you hear nearby? What sounds are in the distance? Describe all the details like you are right in it and experiencing every precious moment. Yes, Sunshine, it can be that amazing!

After writing the vision of living on your soul path, it's important to end it with a simple phrase, "… or something better," because, Sunshine, it is all about the infinite possibilities! The universe may have amazing plans for you that are literally beyond your wildest visions. This phrase will connect you to that possibility. Stay in tune with your future vision by reading consistently over and over again. You will be astounded at the power of your visualization.

Journaling
Hear me when I say these words, "You are the miracle, Sunshine."

A comforting and safe space you can go to as you explore the miracle of you are the pages of your journal. There is something sacred about the pages that are bound into a simple handheld journal that are just so timeless. Since the moment the Egyptians invented papyrus and began to scribe the stories of their time, the simplicity of ink to paper has been there for the soulful expressions of the moment.

One of my greatest creative living tools is my journal. It's the place where I share all my visualizations and where I speak to my heart voice. I also have journals specific to my creative writing and ideas for products. In fact, my mantra "Create the Space for an Infinite Journey of Possibilities," was birthed in a journal entry in 2015.

That's how powerful your journal can be for you too, Sunshine. It's the place you can go when you want to create space to propel yourself beyond your wildest dreams. Each page is your commitment to showing up to pour out your heart and soul and it is bound by your truth—the miracle of you! Each word strung together, just like the words in this chapter are all there to support you and only you, Sunshine.

Sun, Moon, and Mother Earth
Do you believe in nature, Sunshine? Of course you do!

I believe that nature can have a profound influence in our lives that goes unseen moment by moment. The miracle I want to share is really simple—Our sun is the source illuminating all living things, Mother

Earth is our amazing home that provides all living things what we need to flourish, and the steady moon offers it's moonbeams in gratitude to the sun and our earthly calendar following the twenty-eight-day lunar cycle. There's a whole lot of energy between these three amazing forces of nature that I encourage you to explore and discover how they influence your life. I know you will be eternally grateful for your discoveries.

Sunrise Sister Tribe

This one is pure magic and pure love all wrapped up like a glitter cloud bursting all around you. The journey to your soul path and beyond will simply be illuminated by what I love to call the "Sunrise Sister Tribe." Just as the sun awakens each day to rise up and shine pure light into the world, you too will awaken each day and be so immensely grateful for the sisters who walk the soul path too. I actually come to tears in some of my quietest meditation moments when I honor the shared experiences, the immense support and complete truth that another soul has gifted me on my journey. When you get to the layer of another's soul and see how pure their love is that they spread into the world, all I can say is … that is the ILLUMINATION that is greater than any other on this earthly journey.

Sunshine, be open to allowing other souls into your journey when their heart voice speaks to your heart voice. You'll know them when you speak the same language of love. And your life will be forever transformed. The co-creation that is shared in this kind of sisterhood is unstoppable and unbreakable. It is through the tribe you will also have a firm footing on your soul path. And on those days you feel unsure, defeated, or just ready to give up … just reach out to one of your sisters. They will pour back into you with that infinite source of love. I also highly recommend that when you find a sunrise sister who is honest and can hold you accountable, make sure you stick with them day-by-day. Having an accountability support net will propel you on your soul path. You can call each other for a quick five to ten minutes each day to share your goals for the day and report in on how the prior day went. Be honest with yourself and your sunrise sister, because it's okay. There's no judgement, just complete support in that moment. You'll find your heart voice can never share a lie with another heart voice anyway. Be open to the treasured partnership that will form from this authentic accountability. You are so worthy of all your dreams Sunshine, and they will be there every step of the way!

Bonus miracle:
Live each day fully present and aware of what brings you joy and miracles. And then that will evolve into your own miracles list.

Oh my great goodness, Sunshine!

The light is so brilliant in this outpouring of all these strings of words on the page. It has been my greatest pleasure that you chose to travel with each of these words. You stepped into our co-created space and you embraced the learning of how your journey can be filled with infinite possibilities.

Are you filled up with ALL the love?

Are you ready to venture on to infinite possibilities?

Yes?

Oh, my heart is full of love, Sunshine.

It's so full because I know you are on the soul path to live so fully in this very moment.

And that's what this is all about, Sunshine.

Your moments, fully ILLUMINATED.

Shine on sister!

ABOUT JENNIFER GRANGER

Jen Granger is a #1 Best-selling author, Speaker, and Creative Living Mentor.

"I believe everyone is creative. Every action we take creates the journey on the stepping stones of our life. When we understand this creative power, we can harness it for a lifetime of being aligned to our soul's truth on the journey."

Over my lifetime, I can clearly connect the dots in all the ways my life was created by me. It didn't just happen to me. I actively participated in creating the life I was living (the good and the not-so-good parts).

Today, I am more mindful as a create my life. I rely on what I call "creative living" practices or rituals like meditation, crystals, moonbeam energy, intentional journaling, visualization, and expressing gratitude. When I am mindful, I support my journey to create the life of my dreams.

Through my daily practice, I discovered that my passion is to share my creative living knowledge with others. It is my deepest joy to fully step into my role as a creative living mentor, so that anyone can create the space in their life for a journey of infinite possibilities.

Follow me on my blog and receive updates on my creations and programs at www.mysunrisesisters.com or email me at jen@jengcreations.com.

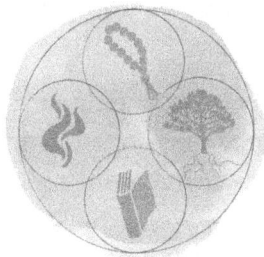

LESSONS FROM THE DARKNESS
FOR LIVING IN THE LIGHT

Jaaz Jones

The power of a story can take us to the darkest space of our imagination or to the brightest light of our desired dreams. The truth is, we all have a story running the soundtrack of our lives. A story that stops us in our tracks, a story that lights us to our highest heights, a story that frightens us, a story that shames us, a story that inspires us, a story that empowers us.

The irony is, one story has the ability to take us to all of these various places within our own life's journey. Our story can hold us in the dark or push us toward the light.

- Take a moment to ponder your own stories and the impact they've had on your life:
- Have you ever considered the stories you tell yourself and where they lead you in your life?
- Have you ever felt stuck – unable to catapult yourself from your limiting beliefs?
- Have you ever asked yourself, "Self, what's the story I'm telling you that keeps me from soaring in my purpose and shining my bright light?"

Inside of our stories are the habits we've established from the stories we've told ourselves. These habits become the default mechanisms of our reactions to our stories. Depending on the habit – some sabotage us, some diminish us, some support us, some empower us.

What are your habits? Where do they leave you and where do they lead you?

Another major component to our stories is the influences we've allowed to infect us or inspire us. The people we surround ourselves with, the environments we dwell in, impact how we hold our space in the world. What we read, what we watch, where we go, and who we spend time with either infects us or inspires us.

What and who influences the story you are living and the habits you've established?

Every story we create, every habit we establish, every influence we allow is driven by one thing – our thoughts. Our thoughts drive our actions, our actions dictate our behaviors, and our behaviors determine our outcomes.

Where are your thoughts driving you to?

If any of the aforementioned questions have piqued your interest, lingered in your mind or sparked your curiosity, allow me to indulge you and share with you my lessons of my Stories, Habits, Influences, and Thoughts that delivered me from the darkness to living in the light.

In other words, (in case you haven't caught the acronym yet): how I shifted my S.H.I.T.

MY STORY

Every debilitating story I've ever told myself began with one of the following opening statements: I am not, I can't, I should … !

I am not enough.

Now this one right here takes up a whole lot of story that gripped me into limiting and disempowering beliefs. First of all, starting with enoughness leads to a comparison which is always a danger zone for living in the light. Mine started around four-years-old when my mother was combing through my thick, curly, kinky mane. One of her girlfriends who came over for coffee and complaints commented, "That girl has got a lot of hair on her head. Too bad she didn't inherit your 'good hair'." Alright, some of y'all know what I'm talking about. A major distinction of beauty for little black girls – the difference between 'good hair' and 'bad hair'. The closer to wavy straight with no curl or kink – good hair. Tight coils of curl – bad hair. Also known as happy nappy hair. I fell somewhere in the middle zone which in comparison to my mother's kinkless curl and soft waves was NOT GOOD ENOUGH!

Not light enough! In the multi-shades of the black folks, I would pass what was known as "the brown paper bag test" by the blink of a shade. Too much sun might just push me over that line. Light skinned, but not fair skinned. Of course, compared to my fair skinned mother, who was at least a shade lighter, I was NOT LIGHT ENOUGH!

Not pretty enough! Though considered a somewhat cute little girl, in comparison—because I could have been lighter, could have had better hair, didn't look white enough, didn't look black enough—I bought into the belief that my medium complexion, my middle space was not enough for good enough. This story ran in the background of my self-image. It also served as my driving force to disprove the self-judgment and the judgment I bought into handed down from others – NOT PRETTY ENOUGH!

Not smart enough! Undermining and underestimating my educational achievements; making a 'B' where I should have made an 'A'. Graduating at sixteen while attending college and in high school simultaneously to prove I was smart enough. Yet, still having the judgment of comparison, prompting me to drop out of college in my first year. However, returning with a greater sense of purpose and direction rather than comparison helped to diminish the voice – NOT SMART ENOUGH!

The "I am not enough story" had its spillover into every aspect of my human beingness; rather, it was my physical being, my intellectual being, my emotional being, or my financial being. What I did come to recognize in my not-enoughness, was that my Spirit being was, is, and always will be enough.

What do I mean by that? Not being pretty enough, smart enough, strong enough, or rich enough are comparisons of my egoic self – my Shego. My Spirit self has no comparison. It is that Spirit self that raises me up out of my own darkness to assure me I am enough, because I am.

Not being enough as a wife, as a mother, as a friend, as an entrepreneur, as a woman have been the spillover from that identifiable moment as a little girl that I bought into a bill of goods that something about me was not "GOOD ENOUGH", and it hovered over me like a cloud but also led me to find my light within.

However, the lessons learned from "I am not enough", like all of life's lesson, are not linear, nor are they a one-time learning opportunity.

MY HABITS

The stories I told myself led me to create certain habits. Some good, some not so good, and some downright debilitating. Procrastination, avoidance, day dreaming, emotional eating, and shopping are some of my core depleting habits.

I'll address the emotional eating because, again, it was based on a story where the seed was planted when I was a child. My mother married a man when I was seven-years-old. The marriage took place approximately six months after a S.E.E. (Significant Emotional Event) in our lives. The event was my first time in a courtroom where I had to identify the man (my babysitter's boyfriend) who molested me. My mother completely broke down and became hysterical. The court room event was even more emotionally impacting than the molestation itself.

The new stepfather my mother acquired came into my room late one night and began fondling my body. The next day, nothing was said. We carried on like it was any other normal ordinary day. I got up, went to school, did my work, played with my friends and came home. However, the day was anything but normal and ordinary. When I came in from school, I made a grilled cheese and bologna sandwich, grabbed a gallon of chocolate chip ice cream out of the freezer and a big bag of Cheetos and commenced to ingesting every morsel until every bit of the ice cream and every chip in the bag was devoured. After eating the whole thing, I went directly to the bathroom and purged every bit of it. No, I had not been informed, nor had I ever heard of binging and purging. It was an automatic reaction to the emotions I was attempting to bury and release simultaneously.

The habit of emotional eating would not impact me until much later into my adult years by attempting to avoid emotional upsets or deal with what I believed to be overwhelming challenges in relationships.

The habit of emotional eating led me to explore the benefits of Emotional Freedom Techniques (EFT) and other modalities to create habits of healing like running, meditation, journaling, and fasting. These have since become the practices I've incorporated to bring me back to dwelling in my light. The interesting dynamic of changing a bad habit to a better habit begins with changing our focus of our desired outcome with each and every breath we take.

MY INFLUENCES

Every encounter we have has the ability to influence us. My mother is one of the most impactful influences that guided the trajectory of my life, both negatively and positively. It was because of my mother's nervous breakdown that occurred when I was seven-years-old and her bipolar diagnosis that I was inspired to become an Inspirational Speaker, Energy Empowerment Coach and Transformation Specialist. Jim Rohn, one of my mentors and teachers once said, "You're the average of the five people you spend the most time with." These are our greatest influencers. By the way, those influences don't have to be face-to-face. Who we watch on the internet, the authors we read, as well as the people we share our space with, all influence us. I've been very fortunate to surround myself with individuals and resources that have made a tremendous positive impact on my life. There have also been choices I've made that have not served my best interest. One of the greatest lessons I learned regarding influence and the ability to create healthy boundaries came from Jack Canfield, one of my greatest inspiring influences. Whenever I am compelled to choose someone else's agenda over what works better for me in my life, I am reminded of Jack Canfield teaching me the lesson, "This is not against you, this is for me." Every relationship in my life has brought forth a lesson and a blessing. Even the relationships that came to an end transformed into a different purpose or simply moved in another direction; all carry the gift of wisdom and growth. The wisdom and growth come from my willingness to surrender up the question, "What (who) is the thing for? What's this relationship, person, moment here to teach me?"

MY THOUGHTS

Everything begins and ends with a thought. In the middle are the feelings reacting to and flowing from those thoughts. By the way, all of the S.H.I.T. you just read was all created by my thoughts. My mom would say to me as a child, "You are not what you think you are, but what you think; you are." There's a line from *A Course In Miracles* that says, "We are much too tolerant of mind wandering." Let's face it. In life S.H.I.T. happens. How we respond to it is what determines our outcome.

One of the most impactful moments in my life where I took ownership of my thoughts was around my mothers' death and the subsequent events that followed regarding her estate, most specifically her townhome.

After my mother's death in 2001, I began running and writing as a cathartic means of dealing with my loss. Running was that free space where I could flow with my thoughts and cultivate my story *In My Mother's Voice*. All I thought about while I was running were conversations with my mother and the life lessons I learned from her. In the meantime, I was still struggling with the resolve of my mother's estate and maintaining her townhome that had tripled in payments due to a senior program she had benefited from. My employee exit package from the airline company I worked for kept me afloat, however, the legal fees for my mother's estate were causing me to sink, quick and fast. Mama's townhome was the last thread of attachment to my past, to my story, to my madness – to be released. As much as I fought to salvage her estate, I already recognized it was time to let go, let God, lift up, and move on.

The night before my court date to learn my fate of the reversal of the increase by the mortgage company, I had a dream I called "the bike". In this dream I was riding my bike on this beautiful, crisp spring day. The sun was warming my skin as the breeze blew over my face keeping me cool and refreshed. The landscape around me was breathtaking. Lush green trees lined the roadside as the billowy clouds brought a cool crispness to the ride. Then, in what seemed like a split second, I was on a rapid downhill race to the bottom, and I had no idea of its end. Suddenly, I was in total darkness, engulfed in a body of water that appeared to be an endless lake. While treading water with my left hand, I was holding onto the bike with my right hand. In a moment of complete and utter exhaustion I looked up into the darkness and cried out, "What do I do?!" I heard a voice reverberate back to me, "Let go of the bike!" Duh! Now, you may quibble that was the obvious. But my realization in my awakening hour was let go of the townhouse! It was changing my thinking around my attachments that gave me a new-found freedom. My ability to live in the light came from my willingness and commitment to manage my thoughts. It's the 100% responsibility that Jack Canfield speaks to in *The Success Principles*. I let go of that townhome, packed all of my possessions into a storage unit and ran my way into my first marathon in Kona, HI. That was the beginning of my journey to live fully in the light.

My thoughts now begin and end everyday with gratitude. Gratitude is the greatest energy that will open up the floodgates of light and lift the darkness from our minds. I am grateful.

"I Am" are the two most powerful words that speak us into existence. Whatever follows "I am" is our declaration of the reflection we choose to light upon the world. I choose love, I choose gratitude, I choose joy!

I Am THAT, I am.

It is now your turn to shift your S.H.I.T. Take a moment to reflect on your Stories, Habits, Influences, and Thoughts that have held you in the darkness. Release your own personal declaration to bring forth your light and declare:

I Am _____.

ABOUT JAAZ JONES

Jaaz "Energy Mogul" Jones, Inspirational Author & Speaker, Transformation Specialist and Energy Empowerment Coach, is on fire for helping mothers and adult daughters transform their relationships into empowering sisterships. Jaaz is the President and Co-founder of MaD Miracles LLC; Transformational Training Company, along with her daughter, best friend, and partner, Genia Jones-Hale. MaD Miracles was created to promote and develop self-love, self-awareness and self-empowerment among mothers and daughters through effective communication, critical thinking, emotional intelligence strategies, and personal energy management.

Jaaz has the ability to energize a room into their power and passion. Utilizing the tools and techniques in her signature coaching and training program, the MaD Metamorphosis™ for personal development and the MaDTech Professional Trainer Development aid clients and participants to manifest their desired intentions. Jaaz directs individuals in mastering focused attention to raise their bottom-line and enhance their personal and professional relationships. She presents her programs through a platform of workshops and retreats, principled from her books, *In My Mother's Voice* and *MAD Transformational Guidebook*.

To book Jaaz for speaking and training or learn more about the launch of MaD Miracles' next level training program for shifting your Stories, Habits, Influences and Thoughts to your powerful possibilities of transformation, visit www.madmiracles.com.

Connect with us: Facebook or Instagram @madmiraclesfanpage and LinkedIn @madmiracles.

35

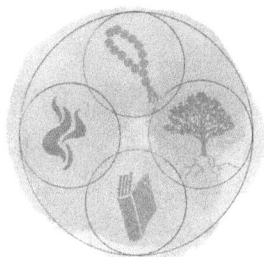

UNLEASHING THE UNDERDOG

Lisa Pezik

I was trained to be an underdog. The message was clear: comply or prepare for battle. If I were "smart," I'd do what Mom said, and if I didn't, I got the silent treatment.

"Lisa, you will not date that boy," I heard, if the object of my affection wasn't white or didn't share my Catholic, American background.

If you take a walk through my old stomping grounds of Lansford, Pennsylvania, you'll find a population of 1,400, and what was once a booming coal town is left with dilapidated homes and businesses gone under.

"Lisa, you'll go to this college and you'll be a nurse. It's a respected profession, and that's what you're doing."

"But I want to be a teacher."

"Oh Lisa, there is no money in teaching. You WON'T do that."

Off to nursing school I went.

I worked three jobs; a nursing assistant; a college campus tour guide; and resident assistant, just so I didn't have to go home and hear "Lisa …" followed by an insult about putting on the "freshman fifteen", or an order as to how I was going to live my life.

But one time, I did go home, and I wasn't alone. I'd met someone. A well-educated graphic designer, a family man with a good heart, a man who wanted children. The only catch: He's from Ontario, Canada.

Before I knew it, we were spending every weekend together and four whirlwind months later, after a long-distance relationship, Eric asked me to marry him.

I picked up the phone to call home and realized that dread, as well as excitement, filled my heart. Not two seconds after I broke the news, my mom said, "Lisa, you will both come for Thanksgiving. I insist this time!"

***

So we go. The football game is playing on the TV and my mom is in the kitchen cutting the turkey with that chainsaw-like electric knife. You can hear that sound from a mile away. That electric knife is probably about as old as me, but it gets the job done. She calls us to the table.

Dad takes his usual place on my right and within minutes is talking about the game and cracking jokes. To my left, Eric is all smiles, but I can't help but think about the future.

"Nobody that wants a future stays in Lansford, Pennsylvania," I thought. I sip on my Cabernet Sauvignon, and I start to dream of our life together. I get so lost in the thought that I don't even realize it's time for dessert.

Eric reaches his outstretched hand to pass me the pumpkin pie and Mom's head whips around.

"Lisa," she shouts, "don't you DARE eat a piece of that pie! Don't you want to fit in your wedding dress? You're going to be too fat to fit into any of them!"

I excuse myself from the table, thinking this is the last time I'll see Eric. He's not going to marry into this.

But later that year, we decide I'm moving. I'm going to break the lease on my apartment, quit my job, and move four hundred miles away to immigrate and move in with Eric, in Canada.

After I'm moved and settled, even though I'm miles away, I continue to make weekly calls to my mom. "Be a good girl and call home," runs through my head, week after week, year after year.

Then we have our son, Oliver, and everything shifts for me, including my priorities.

Whenever my mom said, "Lisa," on the phone, I would just hang up. I didn't want to continue with these weekly battles and directives. I have my own family, my own responsibilities and it took me hours, sometimes days to get out of the funk her calls placed me in.

I start to go to therapy. I throw myself into my family and my work, my RN job, just like I did while I was in college.

Then one day, just as I'm pulling out of the parking lot after finishing my shift, I hear the ding ... ding ... ding of text messages, one after the next. "That's odd," I think.

My first thought is that something has happened to Eric or Oliver. My heart racing, I pull over and check my phone.

MOM.

Text one: Lisa, we haven't spoken in some time, but I want you to know a few things.

Text two: You are heartless.

Text three: You have no soul.

Text four: No daughter of mine would act like you.

I slam down my phone and put the car back in drive. Though my hands are shaking and hot tears are streaming down my face so I can barely see, something in my gut says, "STOP!"

I hit the breaks, HARD. My seatbelt pounds into my chest, it feels like slow motion as I look up. A transport truck whooshes by me, just missing my car. Its horn BLARES.

With my hands on my head, the tears streaming, I scream, "Oh my God, Oh ... my ... God. No. NO. NO. NO. NO. I could have been killed."

I choke back the tears. "I ... can't ... live ... like this ... anymore. ENOUGH. Enough is ENOUGH. "

39

Call it divine intervention, a jolt of life, a brush with death, the pause; it was time to start paying attention to my life.

I couldn't just hang up or call less. I had to do the thing I'd feared the most, and in that moment, I cut off all contact with my mom.

***

Right there, in that car, I thought about my life. I loved being a mom and wife, but nursing didn't light me up. My days didn't light me up. I found my way back to teaching as a nurse educator, but I wanted more.

After I released the relationship with my mom, I released 100 pounds and got every certification possible in health, nutrition, and wellness. I figured since I'd had success myself, I could teach others.

But once I got started, I realized that I wanted to serve people more than just the billable hours for personal training, teaching group fitness classes, and nutrition plans. I was working harder and feeling resentful of the time away from my family.

Online business was something that always fascinated me. Working anytime, anywhere, and I wanted to master it.

I started with an online course and a monthly membership, but I didn't want to promote it to anyone other than my friends and family. In this transition period, I wanted to be visible, but didn't really want to be visible.

I was still working my full-time nursing job and "Lisa, be thankful you even have a job," rang in my head.

"Be thankful for the few sales you've gotten."

Even though I was transitioning into being an entrepreneur that childhood mentality was still winning.

I'd rather have clients and media outlets find me than go out and approach them. It was safer that way.

To help my business, Eric submitted a press release to a local TV station. They wanted to talk to me about my online program as they felt it was unique and noteworthy.

So, I went. The news anchor was cracking jokes with me, and before I knew it, the segment was filmed on live TV and done. I couldn't wait to get home and see the replay!

In the comment section it read, "I'm sorry, but she's a nurse AND a fitness and nutrition trainer. Shouldn't she LOOK more fit?"

A co-worker who saw the segment said, "My husband said, 'cool,' but you don't LOOK like a typical trainer."

I cried for days. I swore I'd never go on TV again. But then I thought about Oliver. I thought about his life.

I thought about all of the people who needed to be reached with my online program, and it sparked a fire in me to serve bigger.

I knew the only way to true freedom was to start loving and valuing my own worth. It was time to be all IN.

The only way you don't win is if you quit on yourself and it was time for me to be a winner. All or nothing.

I started studying under the best online marketers, storytellers, and business mentors. I started getting social media accounts and making videos. With the help of my husband, I launched my website and blog. I built a lead magnet and started growing an email list.

Change takes time, but the decision is made in an instant.

I developed my first online course.

I propped an iPad that a mentor gave me on a stack of books, pointed every light and lamp we had in the house on my face, and pushed the crib to the side in my son's bedroom, as I loved the simple wall paper background. It was the perfect filming location!

I launched that course via a webinar and made a few thousand dollars without it ever being highly produced or perfected.

After the course was finished, I offered a six-month mastermind to the participants and eight people said YES. I only had the first month thought out, but I made a promise and I delivered on it. A winner doesn't stop serving others.

I knew it was time for a podcast. I sat down at my kitchen table, turned on the online program for audio recording and started talking.

I asked if any friends or peers knew how to set up a podcast and a fellow fitness coach offered to help me for free. She loved my work. She told me, "Your work has to reach more people."

I am forever thankful for her belief and help. I recorded and uploaded thirty episodes to iTunes, raw and uncut. After a fellow podcaster commented on the sound quality, I realized that I needed something better. I got a microphone for $100.

Forty episodes in and I realized that I needed a professional intro and outro. Again, I asked around to fellow peers on social networks and I had one made for $100.

Fifty episodes in and I realized that I should be repurposing the episodes and putting them on YouTube, my blogs, and on my social media channels.

Next, I wanted to be a speaker. I started a Facebook and YouTube show and I created a speaker one sheet with the help of a virtual assistant.

I was getting so busy with my content creation that I needed hired help. My assistant started booking me for media engagements and even though the fear of judgement crept in, I didn't let it win.

I no longer look at the comment section. I knew I was a winner when I didn't need the validation of others to shine.

Friends and family started to question, "Why are you working so hard? Your RN job pays so well. Why travel to these mastermind events? Why leave your child to learn? Why are you pushing so hard?"

It gets lonely when you're starting to become a winner by taking control of your life, but there was no going back. There was no dimming the light.

I started to see the value in my work and in my processes. I started to learn from my mistakes and create systematic approaches to content creation, multiple revenue streams, and launches.

I started to get lit up dreaming wild, crazy, unreasonable dreams about serving other underdogs. Those who were told they were crazy, irrational, or stupid, or those who were truly STUCK.

I knew my small team and I couldn't do it alone. I was unsure of who or where the help would come from.

After a mastermind event, I wanted to change some of the content on my website.

My husband and I were mapping out the process of the online business owner and the roadblocks they hit. We identified that once I helped them with the process of content creation, technology was the pothole.

With a glass of wine in hand, our eyes met and we exclaimed, "Oh my GOD!"

I was working my content creation and coaching business separately and my husband was running his creative design, website, funnel, and lead generation team separately.

WE were the help! WE were what we were both looking for!

By coaching together and joining our expertise, we could offer done-for-you services that get established entrepreneurs online quickly. We could shed light on a needed service.

When we bring their idea to light, the client can teach and do what they do best, and we can handle the rest.

We build the website, the course, memberships, funnels. We execute on the content, copy, technology build, launch, and lead generation.

But we didn't want to forget the underdogs just starting out.

We knew our strategy calls were a winner. We'd started offering them, as we are couple-preneurs, to help the rookies avoid the mistakes we've both made. People loved seeing the dynamic of a husband and wife team who parent, play, and work together unfold.

We began to market ourselves together and we knew we had a winning service when we saw the evidence.

We helped an established therapist create her first online course, monthly memberships, sales funnel, and revamped her website.

She told me that she had these ideas in her head for three years, but she was never able to execute, and it ate her up inside.

She was constantly overwhelmed, consuming courses and seminars trying to do it herself.

Her passion is to change how we self-sabotage in relationships and how we raise our next generation. She said that without our help her programs would never have come to light to serve and help others.

Another client who was a health and fitness trainer was being pushed by another mentor to grow her wellness business, but after eighteen months she wasn't making significant income, had a website that didn't convert, and felt misaligned.

With our strategy sessions, we were able to uncover that her spark was creating meaningful parent relationships with tween and teenage daughters and better equipping them to handle today's challenges.

We helped her create a monthly membership program, host events and workshops, and monetize with her blogs and her website. She stated that she forever feels thankful that we lit up the right path for her. This is how she was meant to serve the world.

Whether it was my mom, my own limiting beliefs, or the beliefs of others, I had to do the work of the underdog to get better and win.

My default became:

I am a winner in myself.

I am a winner with my spouse.

I am a winning role model to my son.

I'm going to help others win.

A common trap that stops people from winning is thinking that you have to have it all figured out before you can help someone else, but the truth is, you only have to be a few more steps ahead. You can inspire change in others, which in turn continues the transformation within yourself.

You can turn around, extend your hand and say, "I see you, I hear you. I see the winner in you."

Don't wait as long as I did. Don't wait until you hit your "enough is enough" moment. Don't continue to suffer, thinking that you're not good enough, not smart enough, or you don't "look a certain way."

Don't let the world dictate what you can and can't do. Don't let the critic rule your thoughts. Don't continue to play small. I know you can illuminate your path if you just say "YES" to yourself.

Say yes to those things that light you up. Say yes to the people who champion you. Say yes to that crazy idea that you thought wasn't possible. Say yes to those opportunities that scare you or stretch you. Say yes to your own happiness, health, prosperity, and self-love. Shine your own light so others can do the same.

The winner in you is begging to be unleashed. Set her free.

ABOUT LISA PEZIK

Lisa is a Business Strategist, Thrive Global Author, Worldwide Speaker, and RN who helps you take your business online with excellence. Her strategies and systems help customers connect and become clients, fast!

She's studied under Brendon Burchard, Bo Eason, and Roger Love, and she's featured in Chapters Bookstore with her first book, *Break the Mould*. Her second publication, *The Beauty of Authenticity*, is a #1 Amazon best seller.

Her podcast, "The Lisa Pezik Show", exceeds the industry standard, and she's spoken about online business in the US, UK, and Canada. Audiences say Lisa has fiery inspiration, contagious energy, and to-the-point strategies.

As couple-preneurs, Eric and Lisa specialize in done-for-you services online with courses, coaching programs, funnels, websites, events, summits, and lead generation. Their greatest joy is busting the roadblocks that squirrel brain content and confusing technology create so you can get online with ease.

Lisa is a foodie, a mover and shaker, a ferocious reader, and a soccer mom who lives in Toronto with her husband, Eric, their son, Oliver, and three kitties.

Email: Lisa@lisapezik.com | Website: www.lisapezik.com
Facebook Personal Page: https://www.facebook.com/lisa.pezik
Facebook Business Page: https://www.facebook.com/LisaPezikCoach/
Instagram: https://www.instagram.com/lisa.pezik/
LinkedIn: https://www.linkedin.com/in/lisapezik/
Twitter: https://twitter.com/lisa_pezik
Podcast: https://itunes.apple.com/ca/podcast/the-empowered-life/id1229232466?mt=2
Blog: https://www.lisapezik.com/site/blog
Thrive Global Articles: https://www.thriveglobal.com/authors/8697-lisa-pezik

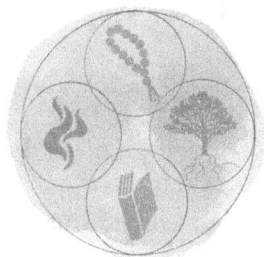

INFINITE LOVE

Samantha Ruth

On my twenty-fifth birthday, Jim blew me away. I'm not at all surprised now, because that's just how he treated me. Always. But at the time, I'd only known him for a month. And yet I knew. That way you just know.

Our night began with just the two of us. I should point out that I'm more a fan of other people's birthdays than my own. But Jim was SO excited to celebrate me, and I felt loved in a way I'd never before experienced. Loved just for being me.

He was bursting with excitement when he gave me my gift. I still have it, like I have everything he's ever given me. I couldn't quite process what I was looking at. It was a calendar, but not just any ordinary calendar. It was a calendar Jim made for me, filled with pictures of me with my family, me and Jim, and me and my fur-baby girl, Harlie. How would Jim have even seen some of these? Gotten copies?

How?

This is how. He secretly called my parents and went to their house. Before I even introduced him, I might add! It was so unbelievably touching, so thoughtful, so Jim.

As if that wasn't enough, he had an ice cream cake (my favorite) adorably decorated with a Peacefrog. Why? Because I get giddy over

47

Peacefrog. It's my favorite song by The Doors, if you're not familiar.

It was more than I could have asked for. Just like Jim. And as we were out with friends in a local hotspot in downtown Detroit, I was just trying to enjoy and absorb it all. Then I heard "bow nuh no" and lost my cool in zero seconds flat.

What's "bow nuh no", you ask? The first notes of "Peacefrog". In a crowded place, on a Saturday night, Jim got the bar to play my (not at all popular) favorite song. My happy song. I was dumbfounded. And one of my four zillion favorite memories is seeing Jim watching me, so incredibly happy just by seeing me happy. Not in the cliché way that everyone is. Genuinely happy just watching me enjoy myself. Like I could see the love beaming from his blue eyes. And that has never, ever changed.

Him wanting to make me happy. Me wanting to make him happy.

That was our life. Every single day. Magic. Our love: magical. That kind of love that everyone around you can just see and feel. And there's so much more to our story. I could tell you hundreds more memories just like these, showing how amazing this dream man of mine is. This man who always brought out the child in me.

The child who was forced to grow up at far too young of an age. That's another story for another time. But Jim brought out that carefree, wide-eyed, hopeful little girl. And all of the issues that little girl had melted away when she saw herself through his eyes.

But nothing in life is that simple or perfect, right? Certainly not me and not even our magical relationship. We were both so young. I had some serious growing up to do and I was focused on establishing my career as a Psychologist. Jim was career and goal-oriented also. (And was in need of some maturing, himself! Let's be honest.) And so, we went our separate ways.

It was the hardest thing I'd ever gone through. Losing my soulmate. My best friend. I'd lost my grandparents, but somehow, we grow up knowing those days will come. But when you dream of meeting your person, you dream of living happily ever after. I'm not sure if I dreamed about that before I met Jim, but I know I did from that first moment on!

So, he went his way, which led him to an amazing life and career in Colorado. And I went my way, resulting in an amazing career in Wayne County, Michigan. A career I wouldn't have had if we'd stayed together, I might add. And we both went on with our lives. Content is the word that comes to mind. We both had everything except love (unbeknownst to the other, of course.) Sure, we each dated other people, but neither of us married or met anyone who filled that void left by the other.

And then I had my next professional accomplishment. I was opening a practice with an incredible partner who was giving me opportunities galore. And being such a wise man, he wanted to market the practice. Here it comes: I was that girl in 2013 with no social media whatsoever. And I was proud of it. Really proud. He didn't believe me at first. Then he teased me. He truly thought it was ludicrous. And then, he tried convincing me. And trusting him, I compromised and created a LinkedIn account.

Wouldn't you know that within a week Jim found me. For real. (And he was quick to point out that I had no social media!) And the rest, as they say, is history ...

It's like we picked up without even skipping a beat. It was as instantaneous as the day we first met. Except it was even better, because we knew what it was like to be apart. We knew not to take a moment for granted. And we didn't.

Fast forward just over three months. It's Thanksgiving weekend in Michigan. Both of our individual traditions included going to The Lions game (I know!) and sharing that tradition has always been really significant for us.

The following day, fifteen weeks to the day after reconnecting, Jim came bursting into my house with that same excitement that he had on my twenty-fifth birthday ... and proposed. I later learned that he had a typical Jim surprise planned, but once he picked up the ring, he couldn't contain himself. That's my Jim. He did, in true Jim fashion, manage to stop at my parents' house to ask their permission, secretly of course.

And he did manage to gather the troops to celebrate. He posted "She said yes!" all over Facebook, something I didn't do because, remember, I didn't yet have Facebook! I thought writing on walls involved markers at someone's house.

And just like that, my new psychology practice faded from view and my move to Colorado was set in motion. Planning our wedding. Planning our future. Living our dreams.

Packing everything and moving across the country would have been a nightmare. But not with Jim. With Jim it was our adventure. Led Zeppelin jamming on the radio, holding hands, with Sassy, my fur baby girl, taking up the entire backseat and we were off. Starting a journal together, planning our goals. And no sooner did we start driving, than our adventure really did begin.

It was a blizzard. I mean one that's still talked about today. There was a major car pileup accident about twenty minutes behind us. And me, crazy anxious, could have completely lost it. But I didn't have to. Because Jim was driving, and I knew I was completely safe. He would never let anything happen to me. But more than that, he knew without me saying a word that I was absolutely terrified. In other circumstances, he probably would've tried to plow through it. But not with me. With me, he pulled off at the first chance he had, and we found a hotel. (Trying to get Sassy to pee in a blizzard was super fun, too!)

In some situations, he'd for sure have been frustrated that his carefully mapped out plan of where to stop, eat, and sleep had been ruined. Not with me.

With me, he laughed about it. I calmed him. We made the most of it. And in some instances, I would have been consumed with anxiety about the following morning drive. But not with Jim. He calmed me. And made everything except our love disappear.

It sounds too good to be true, I know. But that really was us. Losing each other taught us all we needed to know for our relationship. And one adventure at a time, we navigated our way from the highlands to Virginia Village to OUR first home in University Hills.

And plenty happened along the way. The best career move ever for Jim. Plenty of music festivals. Football games. Vacations. My car accident eight days before our wedding. With Sassy in the car. Our dream honeymoon in Costa Rica. Back surgery. My professional journey, which includes the development of my own company, which started as Never Give Up. Nearly two-and-a-half years before I completely knew what that phrase would mean to me.

So much more I could tell you, but what's important for this story is that, in the blink of an eye, I lost it all. I guess we always know intellectually that things like that happen in life, but maybe we just don't think about them happening to us. Especially to me and Jim. After all, we already lost over a decade. This is our fairy tale.

Until it became my nightmare. Jim collapsed at work on a typical Wednesday. And my life has not and will not ever be the same.

From the second I got the phone call, through the memorials, and even for months after that, I felt like I couldn't catch my breath. It was paralyzing. It was four weeks after my major back surgery, and life as I knew it was gone.

Jim was gone. Sam, as I knew her, was gone. My faith, gone. Dreams, are you kidding me? Looking back, I was living in a fog. Correction. Surviving. Living is definitely not what I'd call it. I had friends telling me when to sleep. When to eat. I think that if I didn't have to take care of Sassy or my back, I might not have gotten out of bed. Ever.

Everything became so much more complicated. Simple things were far from simple. And my anxiety was indescribable. About anything. And everything. And it didn't help that the world was full of judges, telling me what I should and shouldn't be doing.

I pretty much felt like a child, learning everything all over again as if for the first time. Internally, there was a tornado, but I was going through the motions that were expected of me. I made a million mistakes along the way. But I did it the only way I knew how.

About three months after Jim passed, I made one of my first decisions since losing him. Which was a really big deal to me. And boy did I catch hell for it from some people I thought mattered. (Talk about ups and downs.) Trauma teaches you a lot about who really knows you and who is really there versus who just says they will be.

I wouldn't be here without the people who really know me. The ones who knew what I needed even when I didn't. While some were telling me what I should have done, my circle was keeping me from drowning from comments like, "At first, I understood, but by now I expected more."

By now? Three months? I felt guilty that comments like this were infuriating me, and then someone in my grief group put it into perspective. "By now? You're a fetus in this life sentence you never asked for and no one knows what's right for you but you." Yeah!

I left that meeting with a newfound commitment to myself. I made the decision to grieve my way, no matter what anyone thought! And for the first time, I could breathe. Just a tiny bit. But enough to give me hope. Enough to begin to see the light.

And the world did continue to judge. Why are you still wearing your wedding ring? Why aren't you back to work yet? You should get out more. And my favorite: … if you can live with your decisions.

But you know what? It no longer mattered to me what anyone thought. Perhaps for the first time. I did what I needed to do, including a lot of just enjoying Colorado with Sassy. I had been so anxious driving after the car accident that this was really a great way for me to push past that fear. I stopped worrying about what others said I should be doing and started taking care of myself.

And I wound up in Grand Lake for our anniversary, where we got married, my favorite place. It turned out to be the most pivotal week of this journey. It led me and Sassy to get another puppy. It led me to a medium. It led to working with Jack Canfield, which honestly has changed my life in the first few months alone. It led me here, to this community of incredible, supportive women where I can share my story of healing my way. Which it turns out isn't just about grief. Turns out, it's all about finally accepting and loving myself exactly the way I am. The way Jim has always loved me. But a way that I don't think I ever have loved myself.

And I learned two giant things.

One: others don't like watching us suffer. They want to fix it. Or maybe they want to fix us?

Well, guess what? You can't fix this. And I won't just pretend I'm fine. I need to feel my feelings, even if that's uncomfortable for others. It's the only way I'll heal.

And two: we don't need to be fixed. We need to learn to accept and embrace ourselves exactly the way we are. And exactly where we are. And for me, that's a woman who lost her soulmate after finally finding him again. And that's a woman with anxiety, anxiety that has gotten worse through this loss. And that's a woman who has never felt good enough, except with Jim.

I put others' voices and expectations out of my head and listened to myself, something that hasn't always been easy for me. And I decided that I'm not enough. I'm more than enough, just as I am. And I'm worth investing in myself and my recovery. So, I am! And I'm allowing it to unfold organically, without obsessing about the whens or the hows (something that has taken a great deal of work on my part and has been worth every second of it!)

So, to all of you struggling out there, please quiet the noise. We're not alone. We will get through this. And it starts by listening to your own voice. Loving yourself. Accepting yourself. And my journey is far from over, but I can tell you that things began changing the moment I shut my ears and opened my eyes! Not only could I see, I could see the light and I could see myself through Jim's eyes: the girl who doesn't just see the light, she shines brightly. And I decided in that moment to BE the light, to illuminate myself, others, and this world through sharing my story and helping others find their light and letting themselves shine.

Just the other day, I heard "bow nuh no". You know, the first notes of "Peacefrog". And I got that excited feeling, the one Jim loves so much. Followed by this moment of clarity, this realization that nothing will ever be as happy, as fun, as joyful ever again without him by my side. And then I had a second moment of clarity: while things will never be the same, I now see opportunities to be happy in a different way. I see new ways of finding joy. Because Jim is always with me and has guided me to a path of being able to illuminate the world. It's the only way I've survived. So, I resumed my goofy dancing and singing. And it hit me … I'm still that wide-eyed girl he loves so deeply, bopping around to my happy song. And now, because of him, I love her too.

ABOUT SAMANTHA RUTH

Samantha Ruth

Author, Psychologist, Trainer, Transformational Speaker & Coach.

Are you feeling overwhelmed? Lost? Stuck? Alone? Maybe even Helpless? I have visited all those places—some more than once—and I know how you feel. My name is Samantha Ruth and I am here to help you.

I have made plenty of bad decisions and I have had some pretty bad luck. I know what it's like to feel like your life has been shattered into tiny, unrecognizable pieces. More importantly, I know what it takes to put those pieces back together so you can live your best life—as Your True Self. I have spent years figuring this out, so you don't have to wait so long.

I am a licensed professional Psychologist, and I am certified as a trainer in Jack Canfield's Success Principles and Methodology. This powerful combination, along with being a graduate of the school of hard knocks, allows me to help you in a unique style, tailored specifically for you. If other methods or professionals don't work for you, let's play this game together and see how we can pick up your pieces and get you unpuzzled.

To connect:

Samantharuth.com
Wholelottalovefoundation.com

https://www.facebook.com/samanthamruth/
https://www.linkedin.com/in/samanthamruth/
https://www.instagram.com/samanthamruth/
https://twitter.com/samanthamruth

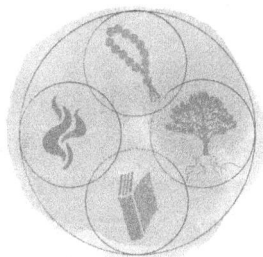

GIVING HOPE

Amy Broccoli

Growing up in the Midwest was a lot of fun. I played outside from dawn to dusk, even in the cold North Dakota winters. Okay, so I probably played outside for an hour in the winter, but you get the point. Born and raised in the Midwest, I lived in North Dakota, Wisconsin, and Illinois. I landed in the suburbs of Chicago in seventh grade and called that my home for many years. Chicago is and always will be my home, even though I have not lived there in over fifteen years. I had my first son in Chicago, I met my husband in Chicago, and I spent my twenties in the city, let's just say "figuring myself out" and leave it at that.

I have never been someone who took the easy road, the ordinary one, the one that my parents probably wished I had. I was a hyper child with way too much energy. I never really fit the norm and I drove my parents crazy. I grew up playing sports. I was a dancer and soccer player. I have been an athlete since I can remember. I have made huge mistakes and had some absolutely amazing triumphs. I partied way too hard, I failed college classes, I attended six colleges, I graduated at the top of my class when I finally did graduate, I had a son at a young age, I was a single mom, I married a great guy, and through it all I always knew God had big plans for me. It just took me some time to actually listen.

I met my husband, Marc, while working as a manager at the Rainforest Cafe in Downtown Chicago (thank you Tim.) I was a single mom at the time and I honestly was not looking to date, let alone get into a committed relationship, because who was going to love my son as much as I did? But I went on the date anyway. I had no idea what God was planning but after that date I knew that Marc was going to be in my life for a long time. We started dating shortly after that and I eventually let him meet my son, Marco. I would love for our story to be all rainbows and butterflies; however, it is everything but that.

I was a young, single mom living in a big city, working crazy hours, and I wanted to get out of the restaurant business, so I decided that I should move to Omaha to live with my mother until I could get back on my feet and finish college. Marc and I decided to give the long-distance thing a go. It was hard, like really, really hard. I got a really good job in Omaha and went back to school. Marc was living in Chicago, the city I loved and missed so much, and I was a little jealous of him. His visits became fewer and farther between, so we decided to break up. A few months passed and one Sunday, as I was sitting in church, I heard God's voice say, "I am not done with you and Marc," as the U2 song "I still haven't found what I'm looking for" was playing. Later that afternoon, I called him, and he came to see us the next weekend.

We wanted to be together. Since we did not do well in a long-distance relationship, we decided that I should move back to Chicago with Marco and I would continue my school there. Those were probably some of the best times we have ever spent together. We lived in a small apartment on the south side of Chicago. I was attending The University of Illinois at Chicago, Marco was thriving in pre-school, and Marc had a great job. We lived simply yet happily. Then Marc was offered a job outside of Cincinnati, Ohio—one we couldn't pass up.

Prior to moving away from the city yet again, Marc proposed to me. It was official—we were getting married. The three of us moved to Mason, Ohio. It was a quiet, little Midwestern town and I really missed the city life. I would go back and visit my friends at least once a month, not really giving Ohio a chance. The small cracks began to form in our relationship. I did eventually get a job (I was still in school) and made some amazing friends. They convinced us to get married in Ohio, so that's what we did.

We lived there for about two years when Marc's company announced it was going to relocate to Chicago! I was beyond thrilled. Unfortunately, there was a "but"—a big one. Marc was given the opportunity to run a company on the east coast, New Jersey to be exact. I said no a million times, but he really wanted this opportunity. And who can blame him? The president of a company before he turns forty? Yeah, I get it. To say the transition to east-coast-living for a girl from the Midwest was a tough one is an understatement. I literally felt like I moved to another country, *and* I was pregnant with our second son. I was sick, lonely, and missed my old life. That's when the resentment really started to grow and the cracks in our relationship grew bigger. I resented Marc because he didn't get it. He got to go to work every day, not sit in an empty house. His career brought us here and I was sick, pregnant, and not doing anything. I was living what felt like *his* life, not *mine*, and definitely not the start of a life together. We moved to a small town where everybody knew everybody, and it was really hard to make friends. I was lonely, sad, and depressed. Marc and I fought all the time and I began to withdraw. We had our second son, Nicolas, almost a year after we moved to New Jersey.

When Marc and I met, I explained to him that I would never be happy being a stay-at-home mom and that I would need more. (I am in awe of my friends that do stay home with their kids, they are the true heroes!) The problem was there was nobody to watch Nicolas if I went to work. So, I became a stay-at-home mom. My resentment continued to grow, really causing a major break in our relationship. We started marriage counseling to try and fix what was broken. We found an excellent therapist who really broke down the issues and we did some work, but it was not enough. I eventually went back to school and graduated. I made some absolutely amazing friends that are now my family. It is really hard to make friends in New Jersey, however, once you do, they are your friends forever. I then began my coaching career coaching youth soccer, then I traveled, then I coached at our high school. I finally felt like myself again, but our marriage was completely broken.

I started yoga and moved onto CrossFit about five years after we moved to New Jersey. I had finally found the place where I felt at home. I had left that inner athlete back in Chicago and I missed her. I began to put the pieces of who I was back together, but still neglected our marriage. It got bad—like really, really bad. We started a business on an already broken foundation, which ended up putting a bigger wedge between us. The business was in the industry Marc grew up in, so again I felt that I was living his life, not mine. The business eventually shut down. It was just too much for us to handle and we were out of money.

So, I was coaching soccer and CrossFit but was living an empty life because coming home sucked. We were sleeping on different floors; our kids were growing up in a house where mom slept upstairs, and dad slept on the couch. It was sad for all of us. We were running out of money; it was all gone. I ended up needing surgery on my shoulder which spiraled me further into a very deep depression. It was my last season as a soccer coach, and some of the girls I coached from the time they were very little were now high school seniors. I thought I did a really good job of hiding my pain, but they were smart. They kept me going, even though it was my job to do that for them. I was drinking a bottle of wine a night and eating countless bowls of Lucky Charms. That lifestyle mixed with not being able to workout led to me gaining a bunch of weight and being extremely unhealthy.

One September night I had had enough. I was done. The bank account was overdrawn for what felt like the hundredth time and I was sick of fighting—fighting with Marc, fighting for my sanity, fighting the bank account, and fighting for survival. I sat in my room with my pain pills from my surgery and was ready to be done living. I started talking to

God, like a real conversation, similar to the way I would talk to him when I was a little girl. In that moment, the moment I wanted to die, a very warm bright light circled me. I heard God tell me he loved me and that my job was not done, that he had big plans for me, and it was not my time to come home. I wanted to argue with him, tell him how tired I was and how I had absolutely nothing left to give. But instead I listened to him and just sat there and cried until I had no more tears left. This was September 22nd, 2015.

That next week I was offered a job suddenly, one that would pay well and give me benefits. I was cleared to workout two days after that. My friend, George, had been inviting me to church for some time, so I decided to stop giving him excuses and go. What's the worst that could happen? I mean I talked to God, right? Best decision of my life. I began to heal my relationship with God, but Marc and I were still broken.

We decided that separating and eventually getting divorced was the healthiest decision for all involved. We did not want our kids growing up thinking that it was normal for their parents to sleep in separate bedrooms. We were both so unhealthy together it seemed like the right thing to do. We told our kids that we would be separating—the worst day of my life—and that there would be a new normal. God then surrounded me with a circle of love and protection that kept me standing through some of the hardest months of my life. (Penelope, Michele, Veronica, Erin, Maria, Abby, and Dana, thank you for making me feel safe and for being my family when I needed it most.) You see, I believe God brought me out to New Jersey so that I could have the best support system in the country, and I will forever be grateful for what these women did for me.

As Marc and I began to figure out how to separate, we realized that we would have to walk away from our house as we were so far into debt. We decided to stay in the house, leaving every other weekend until we could afford to do something else. Again, this did not happen by accident. As time went on, we became friends again. We are huge Dave Matthews Band fans, we got engaged at one of his concerts, it's "our thing" we do with our very close friends, and our wedding song. We belonged to his fan club and happened to get really good seats for both nights he was playing in New Jersey. Leading up to this we had never heard our wedding song live, so I really was not expecting to hear it now. Well, the band played it, and Marc and I were there together. We both cried and something changed in that moment. The next week I was driving home from the grocery store and heard God's voice telling me he was not done with me and Marc, for the second time. For so many years I would ignore this voice or urge, but this time I knew it was for real. I asked Marc to come to church with me and he did. It was the beginning of the healing of our marriage.

We decided to go to a marriage retreat at our church called "Laugh Your Way to a Better Marriage", and wouldn't you know, the speaker was from Wisconsin. God knew what he was doing! During this two-day event we had to look at each other and apologize for all the hurt we caused each other and then forgive each other, essentially wiping clean all of the hurt and resentment we caused. It was in that moment, through tears, that our marriage was saved. We started tithing to our church and our finances began to turn around. We stopped taking each other for granted, taking our family for granted, and began to put the pieces of a truly broken union back together—with God's help this time. Our boys have taken some time to heal, but they are healing, just like us.

God continues to bless us in so many ways. This is not saying that we do not fight or argue, but now when we do, we resolve the issue and move on. I have stepped out in faith with an awesome business partner and I am heading into my second year of owning a weightlifting gym. Marc has had some amazing career opportunities and continues to grow his awesome resumé. Marco finished his first year of college and Nicolas is heading into the seventh grade. This story could have had a very different ending in so many ways, but through it all God was there, guiding me whether I wanted him to or not.

It has taken me over forty years to find my path, the one I am supposed to be on, but God does not do anything by accident. I realized not too long ago as I was walking through the Philadelphia International Airport, on my way to a National Weightlifting Meet with happy tears running down my face, that I am finally where I am supposed to be, doing my dream job. Had I made a different decision that September evening, I would never have known true happiness and would have hurt all of the people I love so very much. Today, I am a coach, an athlete, a mom, and a wife, and I'm damn proud of the road I took to get here, as crooked and uneven as it was. In the end I hope my story shows that you should never give up and to always have faith, even when it seems there is no way out.

ABOUT AMY BROCCOLI

Amy Broccoli is an entrepreneur, wife, mom, coach and athlete. With over twelve years of coaching experience, as well as many years as an athlete, Amy helps athletes of all ages realize their true potential through strength training as the co-owner of Red Panda Strength in Mt. Ephraim, NJ. She is a Level 1 certified USA Weightlifting coach and a competitive Masters Weightlifter at the local, national, and international level.

Amy is also one of the co-creators of Inspired Purpose, whose mission is to show that by lifting each other up the world can be a better place. They do everything from public speaking events to their own podcast, which showcases stories of faith, love and positivity.

Amy, Marc, and the boys still live in West Deptford, NJ, and regularly attend church at True North Church in Mantua, NJ. Amy loves living in New Jersey and no longer thinks it is a foreign country.

To learn more about Amy head over to:
www.redpandastrength.com or
@coach_broccoli on Instagram

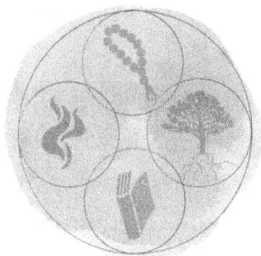

EVOLVING JOURNEY

Victoria Chadderton

As I start this journey with you on these next few pages, I wish I could tell you at the end "and she lives happily ever after!" The truth is, I am always evolving and forever changing. As the saying goes, "The only thing constant is change."

For as long as I can remember I was always trying to become what I felt others wanted. I did not like to have conflict around me and therefore if I conformed then there would be not conflict. I have always been the type to sit back, watch, and learn. I did not grow up with siblings and my extended family were older than I, and so that left me to my own devices to learn the ways of the land.

Television played a huge role in me trying to figure out the world and what culture accepted as the norm and how we were to act. Looking back, I enjoyed the shows that had lots of people connected and loving each other. Conflict was always resolved with the half an hour. I grew up watching *The Brady Bunch*, *Eight is Enough*, and *Facts of Life*. I longed to have a close-knit family even if we were not related, such as in Facts of Life. Oh, how I remember as a child wanting to have siblings to grow up with. Knowing that I would not have siblings, my dreams became of what my future would hold. I wanted as many kids as I could have. I wanted a home that all my kids and their friends would come to and hang out. My home would be large and filled with laughter and love.

In school I wanted to have friends but found it difficult. I tried so hard to fit in and I think that was part of the problem. Kids can see if you are being authentic or not. I would sit off to the side and try and figure out how I could fit in. I was awkward and did my best to conform to what I felt was expected. I was always the kid that was picked last when choosing teams. I was a sensitive child and the bullies could smell that a mile away. I learned quickly how to fade into my surroundings and not be seen.

In high school, I did find a group to call my own. Drama! Go figure, the kid who didn't want to be seen, was up on stage if front of the whole world. Do you want to know the secret? When I was up on stage, that wasn't me! I was the character that I was playing. Those weren't my words; my peers were not laughing at what *I* said but what the *character* said. I did not take my peers' reaction to my character personally. That was my protection. I learned that I could wear these characteristics when I wasn't on stage. These characters became my invisible masks.

I became great at wearing invisible masks. I would become who I felt people wanted me to be. I became great at playing the character of the "perfect" daughter, wife, and mother. I would take what other people defined as success and was killing myself to try and live up to those "expectations". I became numb to my true self. All those little-girl-wishes and dreams were only a distant memory.

I got married right out of high school. I knew that I wanted a family! A BIG one. Oh, I had huge expectations of myself. By the time I was twenty-one, I was married, we had bought our first house, and I had my first son. I was living my dream, or so I thought. Along with that came the financial stress, postpartum depression, and two people who were still trying to figure out who they truly were.

I found myself going through life just reacting to what was happening. The best thing was having two more sons. One of the worst was my husband being diagnosed with cancer. He was thirty-four and was diagnosed with Stage 4 thyroid cancer. Suddenly, not only was I being mom to three amazing humans, but in an instant became a caregiver and provider for my family. This did not match my expectations that I had for myself. This did not match *The Brady Bunch* lifestyle that I had envisioned for myself. Now, I know you are thinking, "That is a TV show. Snap out of it you must live in reality."

My reality was that I was living my life according to what I thought everyone else expected of me. I didn't discuss anything with anyone. I didn't allow myself to acknowledge what my true authentic self wanted. I was afraid that if I did, then I would be rejected, exiled, and voted off the island!

I realized that I had become numb. I was going through the motions to get through the day. Sure, I was functioning, getting through life. But is this how I wanted to be? I wanted to feel the JOY of seeing my sons experience life through the eyes of a young child as only children do. I wanted to feel the excitement of experiencing new adventures. I even wanted to feel the disappointment of failure. I just wanted to feel again.

One thing I have always been able to do is keep my spark of hope ignited and know that tomorrow is another day. For the next five years, I worked on my education, going back to school and obtaining my degree as a psychology major, while raising my boys and caring for my husband. He did eventually get well enough and went back to work. We decided that for the good of the family it would be best if we divorced because we wanted different paths for our lives.

I started going to transformational retreats, workshops, and seminars. I found my tribe and in doing so I started to find my authentic self. I was like a sponge, soaking up all this information. I would read all the books that Oprah would recommend when it came to self-help. Some would click and others would just go over my head. I realize now that what landed was what I needed at the time. I will go back now and reread some of those books that were a blur the first time and get something out of them.

When my kids were little, I would sometimes be up late at night and those wonderful infomercials would come on. One that particularly stood out to me was the guy that was larger than life, jumping up and down on the stage and had this huge white toothy smile. Tony Robbins was trying to awaken the giant in me. I liked what he was doing, helping people achieve their dreams. When I would tell people that is what I wanted to do, they would look at me and say that I did not have what it took to be Tony Robbins. I know they saw me as a quiet person, not as someone who could get on stage and get people jumping out of their seats to walk on fire. Deep down I knew that I did not have to be a "Tony Robbins". I could be my authentic self and still make an impact.

Through self-discovery, I dove deeper into the values work. I found that our values are what keeps our internal barometer intact. When we are living our values, our true authentic self can shine. This took lots of effort on my part to even get in tune with my values. I had become so numb to what I felt. You know how people say follow your gut instinct? I had turned that off so long ago I was sure I would never find it again. As I worked on it, I would try and notice even the slightest change in my thoughts or feelings. When I would feel joy or catch myself smiling, I would evaluate what it was that I was doing in that moment and was this activity tied to a core value in some way?

I am sure that you can guess that family is high on my values list. Spending time with my sons and now also daughter-in-law and grandsons brings me joy. Time stands still when I am playing or reading books with my grandsons. I enjoy creating memories with them.

As I continue to study and work with others defining their core values, I find that when living your values, you live with internal harmony. When our values are challenged, this causes discord and turmoil. I can't tell you what a relief it was when I was able to authentically express those values. This took time to learn. I would go back to wanting to please others, but by doing so, I was dimming my light. Through my struggle I help others identify their values. By knowing our values, we can then align our goals and dreams with them.

Vision boards are a magical tool in helping with this. I have been creating vision boards all my life. I just didn't know that was what they were. Remember when I said growing up I had these dreams? Well they *did* come true. However, I was not clear and perhaps they did not always align with my values. When what I had envisioned came to me, it was something that I had felt others wanted for me, not what I truly wanted. I had this empty feeling. Now I create my vision boards and notice that when I place something on the board and it is in line with my values, the dreams manifest much more quickly.

The best feeling comes when I help others create their vision boards. I remember a time when my friend was having a struggle in figuring out her career path. She was in a job that she liked but it was not bringing her joy, and it required long hours for not nearly enough income. As she worked on her vision board, she grouped the photos into areas of her life, family, career, finances, fun, etc. She had cut out a phrase from a magazine that said "time for change". As she would rearrange the pictures, this phrase kept ending up near the career section. A few weeks after she created this vision board, she was offered a new job with better hours that increased her income.

I have come to the awareness that I am forever evolving and my journey continues. The best thing is I know I am in control of how my story will unfold. I can envision the life I intend to live and carry on. Living a life I have created allows me to shine and live in joy!

ABOUT VICTORIA CHADDERTON

Victoria Chadderton is a speaker, trainer, and coach. She is owner and CEO of Chadderton Network. She has a Bachelor's in Psychology. She is also a Certified Cultural Transformational Practitioner, as well as a Certified Canfield Methodology Trainer.

Her passion is helping others create a life they desire. She does this by helping individuals understand how their personal values impact their life. With this understanding they can create more happiness, fulfillment, and success on their own terms. She creates a safe place for individuals to explore their self-identify through workshops, one-on-one consulting, and speaking.

Victoria lives in Washington State and enjoys spending time with her family and traveling.

You can connect with Victoria the following ways:
www.ChaddertonNetwork.com
Facebook @ChaddertonNetwork

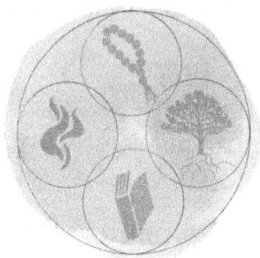

GIRLFUND$

Liz Dowsett

Behind closed doors she quietly weeps
All the while the others sleep.
The money's gone and the house is too
Oh what then can she truly do?

There's nothing more disempowering for a woman than leaving a marriage with no money, no assets, dramatically reduced income, and nowhere to go. It's even more so when you have to rely on your parents, not only for a roof over your head, but to go against everything they stand for in your desperate need and ask them for money—not as a handout, but as a loan to dig yourself out of debt that was incurred by both parties in the marriage but left for you to pay. This is where I found myself at the tender age of twenty-three. To say it was hard is an understatement, and as I look at some of my friends going through similar challenges today some thirty years later with much more at stake, it breaks my heart. Many of them are completely unaware of whose names are on which bank accounts, who has access to the accounts, and how much debt they are actually in. I've only realised while writing my story why I've reacted so emotionally to each breakup as they occur. I've been there, I've experienced it, and I have not forgotten the devastation and upheaval that a marriage breakdown causes. At the time I found it impossible to see how I would overcome the gut-churning agony of starting again, but in my heart of hearts I knew that it was the right thing to do and that one day it would all become clear—just a blip and a memory of what 'was' in the journey of getting to what 'is' now.

Four years of working hard and saving to purchase our first home and we couldn't wait to move in. We'd been renting for four years, far longer than many of our friends, and it was time to join them in the excitement of home ownership. It was 1987 in Australia, property prices were low, bank interest rates were sky high at 17%, which in the world of low rates in 2019 seems simply unbelievable. Like most couples we had our ups and downs but by the time our 'off the plan' home was move-in ready, there were more downs than ups and our marriage fell apart. It was Father's Day when we went our separate ways and the end had been inevitable for quite some time.

The separation began amicably but as we honed-in on our assets and liabilities, it became apparent that we were not going to continue down the amicable path on which we'd started.

Having signed documents with the bank to achieve our dream of home ownership, we were now left with mortgage payments on a house we would never live in. The only option was to sell, so instead of moving into our brand-new home, it was put up for sale. We arranged with the bank to defer all the mortgage payments until the house was sold, so we were keen to settle quickly. Meanwhile, the debt owing to the bank ballooned out above the value of the house and things really began to unravel, because neither I nor my ex had enough funds to cover the shortfall. It was at this point I realised that I would have to come up with the money on my own or declare myself bankrupt.

It was a time of great distress. Becoming bankrupt meant I would have financial restrictions for years to come, and yet approaching my parents for a loan was equally daunting as they held strong beliefs that you don't loan money to friends or family. I definitely didn't want to disrespect their views and the inner turmoil that followed was incredible, but I plucked up the courage and approached my parents for the money. I took a second job which enabled payments on a weekly basis until the whole amount was repaid. I will be forever grateful for their loan and willingness to go against their principles to trust that I would repay them.

Once I was out of the fog of my failed marriage and the debt to my parents was repaid in full, I decided that I would never get in a position again where I relied on someone else for my financial wellbeing. I moved out of my parents' home and decided to keep my second job to start saving again—my sights were now set on a rental property. It took me another few years, but I finally saved the deposit to buy my own place and felt an amazing sense of achievement that I'd done it all by myself.

Meanwhile I'd met and moved in with my 'now' husband, Mike, and we began to plan our life and saving goals, this time for a family home. The relationship was serious, and we wanted to put down roots. Saving with two incomes was definitely quicker and within eighteen months we'd bought our first home, gotten married, and had the first of our three sons.

In the midst of all this life planning, Mike came home one day and asked if I'd be interested in moving to Malaysia where he would manage an office. I said, "When do we leave?" He was taken aback by how excited and receptive to the idea I was, but why would I pass up the offer of free travel and experiencing life in a foreign country? At that stage I didn't even know where Malaysia was, whether it was a third-world country or what it had to offer a young couple, but I was all-in. Travel has always been extremely high on my passion list and my life has reflected that over the years, having now been to over twenty countries—and still counting.

Moving to Malaysia was an incredible experience, a mix of cultures steeped in richness and diversity. Each month we sent money back to Australia and the mortgage payments reduced quickly due to the favourable exchange rate at the time. With tenants looking after the place, we were also reaping the rewards of another rental property—our family home.

We lived a blessed life with our children in Malaysia but during our time there the original rental property had begun to experience some serious challenges. The tenants constantly ran late with the rent and they were completely disrespectful of the neighbours and our property. By the time we arrived to inspect the place there were holes in walls and doors, stains on the carpet, and the back bedroom window was constantly left ajar to allow their unruly dog to jump in and out at will regardless of the weather conditions. There was mud and muck everywhere. The property market in the area was stagnant and it was costing more than it was earning. It was time to re-evaluate and get out, so we removed the tenants, renovated, and sold. There certainly wasn't the profit realised that I'd anticipated, in fact there was no profit at all! After working and saving all that time to see my investment fail was heartbreaking, and it was then I realised I needed to re-evaluate and seek other investment opportunities. This was not a breaking moment—it was a reassess and re-strategize moment. I just needed to be clear on what my goals were and educate myself so I could put action steps in place to achieve those goals. My lesson was clear—I only lose when I quit!

When our children were born, we made a conscious decision that I would stay home to look after them while Mike became the sole breadwinner. But giving up total control of any income-earning capacity brought back many of those gut-wrenching feelings I'd experienced all those years earlier. History had dictated my need for financial independence and here I found myself relying solely on someone else for my financial wellbeing. It's something I struggled with then and continued to do so for many years. Selling my rental property felt like the last piece of my own self from my independent life, but I knew financially it was the right thing to do. It was time to appreciate the support from Mike—for now—and forge ahead together.

I've always been interested in investing and entrepreneurial pursuits, so when our youngest son began school, I embarked on a new journey and started my own virtual assistant business from home. It was a dream job. I had the steady income while working from home with the flexibility that enabled me to volunteer at the school, tend to the children if they were sick, and have a sense of achievement that I was 'back in the game' of work and earning money for myself.

It was around that time my cousin began an investment club, so I was intrigued and eager to be involved. Was this my chance to branch out and create my own financial independence? I couldn't wait to find out. We gathered together a group of women to meet on a monthly basis to discuss investing and investments and each contributed an amount monthly to go into a greater pool of funds. For some the amounts were small, but it still enabled us to invest in things that we otherwise may not have had the ability, confidence, funds, or know-how to do without each other. With my business thriving, this was exactly what I'd been waiting for—connection with others (particularly women), learning by doing, and growing my money.

It was amazing to learn how many investment opportunities were out there other than property, things that I could easily afford to do on my own and also with the club. I was getting my financially-independent mojo back again and I loved it!

Over the years my roles in the club varied, along with my knowledge of investing and investment clubs. It was an incredible learning opportunity. We had a voice, we were all heard, and we made money and lifelong friends along the way.

I created a goal that when all our children finished school, I would take Mike and myself on a European vacation. When our youngest son started school, that trip was still twelve years away, but I had the vision and could see it very clearly. It was going to be our 'graduation gift' to ourselves for raising three amazing young men. So, at the inception of the investment club, I decided that whatever money I grew through the club would go towards our big trip.

During this period of learning and growing my own financial independence, Mike and I engaged mentors for their expert guidance. Learning from someone who has succeeded makes much more sense to me these days than taking advice from those who only have opinions rather than results. It's amazing what gems come from those who have walked a path before you. I have gained great clarity, not only financially but also personally and spiritually by having incredible mentors in my life.

The investment club continued to operate for an amazing twelve years and with that came growth in friendship, knowledge, and of course portfolio value. So, when our youngest finished school, the funds were there ready to go—all we had to do was chart the course of our European vacation, book the tickets, and head for the airport. My dedication to the cause, strategic planning, and my investments had done so well over the years that I was able to gift Mike and myself a two-month holiday where we took in Spain, Portugal, France, Italy, and Greece! As an added bonus I had also saved enough to fly us business class and to extend the trip by another two weeks to take in Belarus. A number of people exclaimed that I was lucky that Mike was taking me on such a wonderful holiday. He would always proudly respond that it was me that was taking us and then follow up with my story of goal-setting and saving. Oh, the joy of knowing that I made this happen for us!

I believe we are all capable of creating our own exciting lives, whatever that means for each of us. It's all about identifying how much we really want something and then making it happen through effective education, creating action steps, and following through to make them happen. And remember, if you think you can't, then you're probably right; and if you think you can, then you're probably right, too. Thoughts and beliefs are powerful and should never be underestimated. I could say going to Europe was the trip of a lifetime, but my life is still going, and I certainly intend to repeat the process. But this time it won't take me twelve years to save, because plans are already underway for the next trip in the very near future!

I believe I have a definite responsibility to myself and my family to be financially educated. I believe it's important for the next generation to learn from our experiences. My children are in their early twenties and they are already investment savvy. It's not about how much you have but what you do with what you have and how to make the most of it. My portfolio now stands at forty investments over a range of asset classes, some of which I'd never heard of when I began my investment journey and some which weren't even invented when I first began! I'm proud to say that my passive investment income now exceeds the income I used to make working hard as a virtual assistant—a goal that has enabled me to discontinue the back-breaking work of being hunched over a computer all day long.

We all make choices about what we do with our money, but do we actively plan on what we want the outcomes to be? What are we teaching our children? What are we teaching ourselves? How financially aware or financially educated are we? Who has taught us in the past about these things, and who can teach us now? For me, financial failure is not an option. I believe in my own resolve. I create my own strength of character and I have complete ownership over my own financial future, regardless of my relationship status.

Success comes in many forms and I am excited to continue to educate and grow to expand my own knowledge as well as to educate and share my knowledge with others. Since the investment club disbanded a few years ago, I've connected with like-minded women worldwide. It's heart-warming to be able to support each other as independent women and I look forward to connecting with many more in the years to come.

Deep inside she knows she'll win
So she picks up her life to begin again.
And so the victory was hers all along
From the inside, bold and strong.

ABOUT LIZ DOWSETT

Liz is an entrepreneur, business owner, investor, mentor, poet, published author, and facilitator of women's workshops.

Over the years her love of travel and adventure has seen Liz jump off mountain tops, climb extinct volcanoes and get up close and personal with snakes and tigers. She loves experiencing all the diversities of life, from camping in the Australian outback to staying in city hostels or hotels and exploring ancient cities and spiritual landmarks worldwide.

Her rich life experiences have been made possible by being financially strategic over the years. She is passionate about other women having access to similar knowledge, regardless of their financial or relationship status. Having successfully navigated a marriage breakdown, financial hardship, investment triumph, and business growth, Liz sees her mission as educating women through fun interactive workshops and online courses based on experience. She has a straightforward, inclusive, and engaging approach and generates excitement and enthusiasm in all she does.

Liz's GirlFUNd$ mantra is:
Be more – of who you can be
Do more – for yourself and others
Have more – so you can give more

Currently living in Melbourne, Australia, Liz is wholeheartedly supported by her husband, Mike, and sons, Evan, Liam, and Troy.

Website: www.girlfunds.com
Email: liz@girlfunds.com
Facebook: facebook.com/Girlfunds

PIECES OF ME

Michelle Eades

O ver the years, I have sought the missing pieces of me, the insights, awarenesses, and knowledge that would help me to understand why I am like I am. In the beginning, I might have had about three or four percent of those pieces … now, my pieces make up about eighty-five percent of me. There are still pieces to find and I also know that there are pieces which are lost forever.

All the Pieces of Michelle which have been gathered bring me to a place where I understand that "I. Am. Amazing!" (I didn't know that I was amazing for the longest time. There was an awful lot of darkness I had to wade through to get to that realisation.)

I am an Oracle Card Intuitive. I love oracle cards and I have sixty oracle card decks on my shelf. Just saying that makes me SMILE. I love playing with oracle cards! I love the different decks with their different themes. I love the artwork. I love that they are so easy to read. I really love that they provide guidance whenever I need it.

Exploring all things 'not normal' or intuitive makes my heart sing. I love choosing my daily card message and using cards to make sense of something I don't understand.

I am also absolutely passionate about exploring past lives. I love finding out where and when I lived before. I love being able to tell the story and garner insights into issues that may be affecting current lifetime experiences. There is a sense of knowing myself more fully because I have discovered insights from the past.

I am grateful for oracle cards and past life exploration. They have been essential in helping me to navigate some of my most challenging life experiences.

I am Amazing! I am living a life that I choose to live. I am strong and rich and filled with JOY ... most days. I am loved, so deeply loved. I have an incredible SMILE (as I am constantly told!) I am psychic and intuitive and made up of hundreds of thousands of stories ... some wonderful, some tragic, some inspired, some dark, and many which don't belong to me.

THE DARKNESS

If you trust someone to do what they say they are going to do or to speak the truth and then they don't follow through, you learn you can't trust that person or that situation.

When you are born, intuitive and highly sensitive, into a family where being in integrity and being truthful are fluid behaviours, you learn not to trust.

If your mother finds herself pregnant and afraid of what your father will say when he finds out so she decides that she needs to miscarry you, the earliest imprint you have is of not being safe.

When you combine lack of trust and not feeling safe, you get my life: a journey filled with anxiety and a constant battle between being fiercely independent and wanting to not exist.

My life runs like parallel paths, one light and one dark. To begin with, the light path was only light on the outside. The dark path was my reality for many years. People didn't know about the dark because on the surface I was light and bright and enthusiastic. Only people I trusted implicitly knew otherwise.

I live with anxiety. Those early life experiences hardwired distrust into the core of my being. Everything I do now is put through the filter of 'anxiety', turned over and over, turned upside down, run through the gauntlet of my inner critic and her team of naysayers and autocrats, and spat out, leaving me heaving with sweat on the other side.

I spent years and years traveling a path without light ... without light that I could see. I spent my days looking inward, attempting to understand why the outside world was the way it was. No matter how hard I paid attention to everything going on around me, I never seemed to see the world the way others did.

Anxiety arrives in the form of extreme fear about doing something new or unusual. Growing up in an overprotective environment where I wasn't allowed to 'go out and experience the world' and where I was constantly criticised for everything I did meant that I missed out on learning essential skills needed for successfully managing everyday life.

When automatic teller machines came into being, I couldn't use them. I didn't know how and the risk of making a mistake and bringing attention to my actions terrified me. It was easier to stay away and not learn. Eventually, a friend showed me and stayed with me the first few times I used one. The same thing happened when I used a carpark with entrance barriers. To get the gate to open, I had to push a button to receive a ticket from the machine connected to the arm. Fear of 'getting stuck', doing something wrong and holding up others in the queue, or not being able to get free of that position was paralysing, so I went to places that didn't use carpark entry gates. Eventually, David, my husband, showed me how to use them.

I watch people to see what the appropriate way to behave is, in any and every situation. I don't trust that the simplest of things are going to be easy for me. I have been known to rush home to use the toilet because I couldn't see a toilet in a restaurant. David usually makes phone calls and organises things, so I don't have to. If I was doing something for my kids, it was easier. Making sure they were happy and safe and

LOVED was my guiding principle.

Even as I was a fearless mother and protector, I was a broken and damaged "Michelle".

I probably suffered with anxiety from my earliest days, but I only realised the reality of it when my mind broke, at the age of forty-nine. That was the darkest point of the dark path. No lights. No awareness of anything in the world around me other than the fact that every insight, tool, and strategy I used to be able to rely on had broken. My outer and inner worlds were completely dark.

I spent days sleeping. If I got up, I only had enough energy for a short period of time.

I barely ate. David would make scrambled eggs for me: one egg and I was full.

I cried. I cried and cried and cried.

I learned that much of my trauma occurred in my earliest years. A psychologist helped me to explore old scars and also gave me the opportunity to really understand why I was traumatised. I lived with verbal and psychological abuse for most of the first two decades of my life.

I have rationalised that period and those experiences of neglect, so that a lot of the time I figure it was 'just a tricky childhood'. Until I have a panic attack, in my car in the carpark, because something caught me off guard or I find myself driving home and hiding in my darkened wardrobe sobbing because I couldn't make the petrol pump fit in my car.

My Brave Self learned to fight. She learned to seek answers to her questions and found people who could help her make sense of her world. I am so very grateful for my warrior-self because, even though it was incredibly hard to face my fears, I did face every single one of them.

I always chose the hard path.

I always chose the most difficult option.

I ripped open my heart and my soul visit after visit, session after session, with my naturopaths, counsellors, psychologists, and clairvoyant readers.

I learned as much as I could lay my hands on about my family story, the past life connections with my family members, my significant past lifetimes, my astrology and my numerology. I signed up for a three-month coaching program and each week I would cry my way through my phone sessions, allowing the emotion to erupt, my body to purge, as I sought strategies I could use to make my journey easier.

With that (and a lot of time), the outside light in my world finally began showing up in my inner landscape as well.

THE LIGHT

I heard of an idea which really captured my imagination. The practice involved telling yourself you were amazing. I loved this! I asked my teenage daughter if she would practice it with me. We spent many months saying to each other, "You are Amazing!" and responding with, "Thank you. So are you." Everything started shifting. It became so normal for us to have this little banter moment together that we started doing it with the people around us. Everyone loved it.

The interesting thing about changing up language, and mindset, is that as you create change the world around you changes with you. What you say is what you attract. As a young person, my most used expression was, "I can't." As an adult with children, I learned to say, "I can." Everything began to change.

When I was young, the only world I knew was filled with negativity, darkness, and criticism. Once I had my family, my world changed and so did the world around me. The aspects of my life which were not in alignment with my mindset fell away.

Who would have thought that such a simple statement, "I am Amazing", would become the basis for everything I do and believe now.

My 'gift' from suffering with anxiety is a need, a desire, to explore WHY I was in this situation and how to navigate through it. In the earliest days, my focus was on paying careful attention to everything around me. What did people say? How did people act? What was appropriate in any given situation? I didn't quite understand, intellec-tually, why this was important. I now know that it was the only way I had to make sense of my world. If I knew the 'right' way to behave then my parents would love me. If I knew the right way to act then I wouldn't be embarrassed in social situations.

As an adult, I manage all of this so much better, yet the inner turmoil I experience leaves me exhausted. I find myself being deliberately pos-itive, uplifting, supporting, nurturing, and enthusiastic—in all social situations—because I never want anyone to feel like I did as a child, and still do as an adult, when anxiety makes you feel socially awkward and very separate from the world around you. I have learned tools and strategies and how-to's for navigating everyday life.

I began offering the "I am Amazing!" experience in my workshops and gatherings. I would watch to see how people responded to it. Some were in complete denial. Others fully owned their 'amazing'. Most fell somewhere in between. The most incredible aspect of this experience was that everyone felt better! Even if they weren't quite ready to accept that they were amazing.

A boy I had a crush on in high school told me that we had known each other before. I was fourteen-years-old and that was the beginning of my quest to understand everything I could about reincarnation and to find all my past lives.

As an adult with two young boys, I had one or two clairvoyant readings a month, for many years, wishing I could do what my Readers did. I felt like if I could just touch the worlds that they accessed so easily something would fall into place within me. I desperately wanted to be able to access my own past lives and find out why things were so difficult in my current life.

When I was thirty-seven, my Reader told me that all would make sense in a couple of years. I grumbled. A lot. I used to grumble often with this gorgeous man who was one of my past life husbands. He would just laugh at me, then take my hand and we'd go out for coffee.

The thing is, he was right! Everything fell into place when I turned forty. Not that turning forty itself made me psychic. No, it just happened to be the time that I had the realisation that I had always been psychic and, therefore, had always been able to access the stories from the past.

Over the next fifteen years, I learned about oracle cards and angels, sought out alternative health care and health management options, and opened my front door to people who were like me: different and lonely. Learning about angels, doing intuitive readings, and discovering my tribe at my first Angel Intuitive Event, showed me how many people in my local area were also in need of finding a community they 'fit' with. I decided to create a space for us to gather, where we could talk about all manner of 'weird' things like spirit guides and angels and animal totems. We used oracle cards, had inspired discussions about the messages and insights each person in the group had 'intuited', and talked about past lives.

I created a tribe. I found people who thought that I was amazing, and who learned that they were amazing, too. One conversation at a time, I turned on a light. One conversation at a time, being different and feeling lonely changed to feeling accepted and being part of something 'more'.

In the beginning, I would periodically meet people who were like me. When I read for them, I could see an inner light shining, oftentimes a light with which they were unfamiliar. I was so excited! We would talk and connect and talk more. I began gathering these people, connecting with them to create what I imagined was a web of energetic light in our world. I invited them to get to know other light-shining people, especially those who were ready for learning how to shine more brightly.

Our tribe is filled with amazing people. They are all seen. They are seen in a way that I was not seen as a child. They are part of a community, in a way that I was not for such a long time. Some have stayed connected, some have moved on. What everyone has in common, though, is their own amazing inner shining light.

Now I access my own past lives and travel the world to find the places

I once lived. I see past lifetimes like movies on a screen in my mind. I work with clients and love the JOY which comes when they have those light bulb moments of awareness, seeing all the pieces fall into place. I love witnessing their mindset shift when an oracle card message or a past life insight brings light into their eyes.

I love being able to hold a light steady so others can find their way to their own 'amazing' selves, collecting their own 'Pieces of Me'.

ABOUT MICHELLE EADES

If there was a course that involved oracle cards offered in Australia, Michelle attended it. A Professional Master Level Soul Coaching Oracle Card Practitioner (Denise Linn), she also explored the worlds of the angels (Angel Intuitive), animals (Animal Dreaming with Scott Alexander King), vibes (Six Sensory Living with Sonia Choquette), and crystals (Crystal Awakening Workshops, all levels, with Rachelle Charman). She is also the creator of the JOYFUL WARRIORS Cards, a deck of 33 Strategies for Managing Anxiety and Living an Authentic Life.

Michelle is passionate about Past Lives, having had more than eighty clairvoyant readings exploring past lifetimes. She learned about previous incarnations with each of her children, her parents and her brother. She has collected information on more than 100 of her own lifetimes, discovering a soul-deep connection with Norway, insights into her past life husbands, and how her family members reincarnate together, often.

Understanding the connections between oracle cards, past lives, and current life happenings is Michelle's favourite thing to do. She loves nothing more than sharing insights with anyone interested in listening.

You are invited to explore Michelle's World at www.michelleeades.com

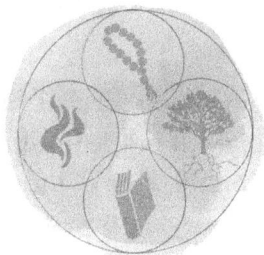

ALWAYS GO WITH THE FLOW!

Brenda Everts

Setting my sights on the financial services industry, I spent many years studying while raising my family, which resulted in the beginning of my financial planning career. I loved financial planning and formed many solid client relationships. I enjoyed the fact that I got to advise clients on how to get from where they were to where they wanted to be. However, at the time, the environment I was required to work in demanded my attention sixty to eighty hours a week. At the same time, I faced the struggles of being a newly single parent to two teenage daughters. I encountered resistance every day, but I continued to persevere and push forward. Ultimately, my health suffered. I was diagnosed with Fibromyalgia, and having struggled with migraine headaches my entire life, I was living a cycle of chronic pain, amplified by stress.

Monthly visits to my physician for many years resulted in a diagnosis that I was not willing to live with. I was getting worse and my physician warned me that I was heading down a path that would ultimately change my life and not for the better. I was facing long term disability or perhaps a cancer diagnosis due to the stress. She blamed my job primarily amplified by the pressure I was under as a single parent. This was my wake-up call. At that point I refused to accept that this was my normal. I decided to make a healthy life choice and left that organization for another. It was life changing. I was finally able to have a good work-life balance. I focused on eating well and getting the right amount of exercise and had my stress under control. I stayed focused on my journey back to health, at the same time building my own successful wealth management practice. To this day my journey to health continues.

It was at this point I felt I had the capacity to assist when a local animal rescue organization was threatened with having to close their doors due to financial difficulties. I decided at least a call to offer my assistance was warranted due to my love of animals and belief in the cause. I approached the organization and was asked to join the Board of Directors. I gladly accepted and looked forward to expanding my knowledge and learning about being a Director for a non-profit agency.

The years of knowledge I had gained working in the financial services industry was a huge asset to the organization. I was able to lead project after project and the organization stabilized. It was a lot of work and investment of my time, but I was passionate about where I could take things and always had many ideas floating around in my head about ways to take the organization to a new level.

A few years later, the organization decided to pursue building a high-volume, low-cost spay and neuter clinic. We believed having such a clinic was crucial for the future welfare of animals in the vast service district. Due to the history of similar clinics and the amount of animals' lives that would be saved, it simply was the "right" thing to do. Integrity told me that this was something that absolutely needed to happen. Under the guidance of another organization with many years of experience with similar clinics, the decision to proceed with the project was made. A successful business plan and a grant application for the cost of equipment for the clinic was submitted and approved by a funder. The community was supportive with donations.

With the assistance of the other organization, the construction drawings were completed and submitted for final approval and financial consideration of support. Things were moving along, and I was confident and excited.

Shortly after the application was submitted, we were faced with a change in our Executive. I was elected as Chair.

As Chair, I worked with the other organization and continued to move forward as it was integral to the future of the clinic. There were grant restrictions to contend with: we had less than a year to turn the project into reality or the grant for the equipment would have to be returned.

Conversations about building a low-cost spay neuter clinic in our area continued. It was determined that the original drawings and price tag for the building were simply out of reach.

I then produced a scaled down version of the original drawings, which all agreed was better and most cost-efficient, and was given the okay to proceed with a new set of drawings. Another request for financial support was to be submitted for approval.

It was at this point when resistance started to appear, and I missed the signs due to the encouragement I was receiving to move forward. I had been working so hard to make things work, and I allowed myself to feel that I had no choice but to continue under their guidance. Perseverance and integrity kept me going even though I was going against the "flow."

All the back and forth with the organization took a lot of time and eventually the grant expired. All communication then ceased. Here we were, with no partner or supporter and an expired grant that was due to be paid back. I recall asking myself at the time, why? It appeared that no matter what I did, I was being met with resistance. I questioned myself on whether this was not something I should be doing, because the Universe clearly was sending out a lot of "red flags" and making this goal very difficult to achieve. My strong core values, integrity and perseverance, screamed out at me every time I thought about just giving up; they kept me moving forward. Giving up would have been what was best for me due to the extreme amount of free time I was dedicating to the project, however the dream of opening this clinic, for so many right reasons, prevailed.

I wondered if there was another way? Did we really have to give up? Could we make use of the existing space we had? I was aware of potential limitations, but determined it was a possibility. I applied for an extension of the grant and submitted new preliminary drawings and a new business plan. Things had to happen fast! While searching online I found a free mentorship program for animal shelters planning to open a high-volume spay and neuter clinic, within guidelines! With nothing to lose, I applied for the mentorship program and submitted the new business plan and a rough draft of the drawings to set up a clinic within the existing space we had. We were approved! The grant extension application was approved as well. We were definitely back in the flow and the future looked brighter.

Formal drawings were completed, the job tendered, a contractor hired. Construction commenced. With two months remaining before the expiry of the grant once again, it was now time to order the equipment. Having a wealth management background in no way prepared me for the task ahead, one that should be taken on by someone with a medical/surgical background. I had no idea this was going to be my biggest challenge. Our mentor provided a list of equipment necessary, but since I no idea what the equipment was going to be used for, it was like reading a manual in another language. This consumed me. However, once again, I persevered because I believed there was no turning back. We had come so close and the stress I was under was immense.

The equipment was on order and construction was winding up. The next steps were to find a veterinarian to run and staff the clinic! Having had a veterinarian to run the clinic from the beginning would have made the most sense, but financially it was not in the budget without any external support. The risk of not finding a suitable veterinarian was huge. I stayed focused on the end result and trusted the Universe that everything would all fall into place. I simply believed it was possible.

We hired a veterinarian who was exactly what we had been hoping for, one with a passion for shelter medicine. At this point all my worries and doubts started to disappear, and it was clear this clinic was going to become a reality!

Once the veterinarian was on staff, certain needs for the future became evident from an organizational standpoint, which included a clinic operation. This resulted in some positions being changed/deleted. As the Chair, you never carry any votes, and these decisions were being made by the Board of Directors. A Chair, however, is the designate to deliver the news of the changes to the staff. New positions within the organization were being offered and existing and former staff were encouraged to apply.

This ended up not going in the forward direction that was anticipated and once again resistance manifested in a very difficult way. Within days of the staff changes, an application for the staff to join a union was sent to my attention. I was on vacation and we were given forty-eight hours to respond. Once again, integrity did not allow me to walk away and let the chips fall as they may. The new clinic was set to open in less than three months and this chain of events would delay that.

Shortly after, I made the choice to resign prior to the completion of the project and near the end of plans for a major fundraiser I had been working on that would bring in the funds to assist with the clinic launch. I believed that the work I had done for the organization had been done selflessly on my part and for the good of all. However, an unjustified claim against me as Chair was the last and final resistance I was willing to face. I was done. Having had a solid reputation that I spent my entire career building was very important to me and I was not going to allow this to ruin mine. It was at this point I realized that completing this project was not my job.

As a volunteer, I realized that the amount of work and sacrifices I had made during my tenure with the organization was serving them, but not myself. Integrity can come at a price, and I had paid that price. The amount of resistance that I continued to face with building the clinic was a key indicator that was blocking the universal flow. I clearly was meant to be doing something else. I had truly believed that this project would not be able to come to completion without me. I was wrong.

Shaken up with this new reality, there were many ways I could have responded. This is where E + R = O, a formula for success that I learned through my Certification as a Canfield Trainer in the Success Principles, became my guide. Any event that happens results in a response, which you have total control over, and subsequently gives you an outcome. Thousands can experience the same event but there will be thousands of different outcomes for the event based on how people choose to respond.

I chose peace, health, and happiness as my response to this event. Had I chosen negativity, revenge, and sadness, I would have been faced with a drastically different and not-so-nice outcome, one that could have consumed me and held me back for years. I chose to move forward, heal, and not look back.

Moving forward, I now can say that I have been given a tremendous amount of clarity about my future which allows me to focus on my life purpose in a healthy and less stressful way. My purpose to inspire and share my knowledge with those who are open to receiving my advice guides me. The extreme amount of stress I was under the last few years was not healthy. Resistance was the reason I should have been more aware when faced with each uphill battle. Any challenges that appear in my life, I will now view as a message to focus on a different direction and reevaluate the journey. Having lived in resistance for so long, I was used to life feeling hard, and I used my integrity and perseverance to fight against the flow. When I look back at my life, I realize that resistance was very predominant in my marriage, my former work place, my family relations, and the volunteer position. I have chosen it to no longer be my normal. This was the biggest gift I was given from my experience with volunteering and it was a life-changer.

Where in your life are you facing resistance? Is life fun and filled with more ease than struggle, a dance and not a constant uphill climb? What is the Universe trying to tell you? Take care of yourself first and foremost. What is meant to be will flow effortlessly into your life without resistance. That is how you will know you are on the right path.

How to move out of resistance and into receiving:

Step 1. Acknowledge what is happening.

Step 2. Acknowledge your response to what is happening and review the outcomes that it is presenting.

Step 3. Acknowledge the possibility that you can move away from resistance and start enjoying happiness, joy, passion, and living a life you love.

Step 4. Allow yourself to feel what that possibility can bring. Do not resist what you feel about the resistance. Practice letting go of it.

Step 5. Take baby steps: always keep moving forward and above all take care of yourself.

ABOUT BRENDA EVERTS

Brenda Everts is a Personal Financial Planner and has graduated from many financial certifications, including but not limited to the Canadian Securities Course, Conduct and Practice Handbook Course, Wealth Management Techniques, Advanced Financial Management Techniques, and the Canadian Insurance Course. Brenda has spent her entire career in the financial services industry and has experienced success in the Wealth Management field helping people establish financial stability and success. She enjoys much fulfillment guiding others so they can achieve their lifetime financial goals.

Brenda's passion for helping others has expanded beyond the financial services industry. Brenda has received professional training certifications with Jack Canfield as a Success Principals Trainer which includes her certification in the Canfield Training Methodology. She is also certified as a Practitioner of Cultural Transformation Tools with the Barrett's Value Centre.

These certifications allow Brenda to coach people and organizations to get from where they are to where they want to be; her certifications also help her identify what a client's core values are and which ones may be holding them back from reaching their full potential and where resistance may be limiting them.

As a coach she creates concrete action plans to move people forward to ensure their success.

Brenda enjoys being a mother to her two beautiful daughters and a proud grandmother. In her spare time, you can find her enjoying time with close friends, paddle boarding out on the lake, or healing her body with Pilates and Yoga. Her learning journey is ongoing.

To learn more about Brenda's coaching work please visit her website at livelovebe.ca

To connect with Brenda: Facebook: Live Love Be Coaching

Instagram: live_love_be_coachingEmail: Brenda@livelovebe.ca

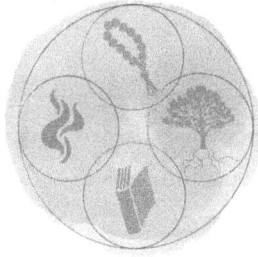

SHINE A DIFFERENT LIGHT

Claudia Fernandez-Niedzielski

It was a cold, February night in Lester, Iowa in 1992 when the world as I knew it changed forever. I was staying with members of the family who had hosted me as an exchange student in 1986. Suddenly, I was awakened by bright lights that begged me to follow them. I ran outside the house towards the church, then ran back to the home of my host family as I desperately tried to escape the voices and steps of those I could swear were chasing me. As I entered the empty house (my host family was on vacation), I made a mess. I removed all the unloaded guns from the gun case; removed all my clothes from the drawers; decided to take a bath and threw pillows, comforters, and sheets out of the window and jumped out of the one-and-a-half story house, fully naked, to escape from the voices. I don't know how long I ran around the small town. They would later tell me that I ended up knocking on someone's door in the very early hours of the morning and that soon after, I was hospitalized. The doctors called it a full-blown psychotic episode; one that would require the use of a straight-jacket, heavy medications, and a padded cell to avoid self-harm and harm to others. The diagnosis (one that would later be changed) was schizophrenia. I cannot begin to imagine what my parents felt when they got that call. What followed was a terrifying and very dark time in my family's life. It would take six more months of hospitalization with 24/7 care by family members, many medication combinations, electroconvulsive therapy, and the board of psychiatry in Mexico City to finally bring me back from the darkness and diagnose me with Bipolar Disorder.

The question that haunted my parents was, "How did this happen?" I had been a healthy child from the day I was born. I was capable of making friends extremely easily, I loved school and was always at the top of my class. I respected my parents and while I was always stubborn, hard-headed, and a little obsessive, there were zero indications that one day they would be faced with the reality they had in front of them. Or were there truly zero indications? Were the signs there all along and we just did not know what to look for and were unable to recognize them?

I had been in a long-distance relationship for four years and the last six months of those four years (just before I traveled back to Iowa) had been extremely hard. Once my parents were informed and understood how Bipolar Disorder is triggered, they knew the indications were there way before I left. I had stopped all social activities with my friends, and I would stay in my room for long hours behind closed doors. I would find myself crying uncontrollably at work, when walking down the streets, and at home in my room. I had begun to make reckless decisions with my relationships, I was spending more money than I had so my credit cards were all maxed out, and I was always in a daze and began to not care about my performance at work. All of these things were indications of a deep, deep depression, one that would cause me to spiral out of control on that cold winter night in 1992. My doctor also found out that a couple of my dad's uncles and aunts had a history of depression and schizophrenia. My parents would learn that mental illness is hereditary, just like many others. This was a huge revelation. The family history and the behaviors I exhibited before I left were all indicators that something was not right. If my parents had known what to look for, things could have been different.

It was 2015 and it had been twenty-seven years since I made a full

recovery from that devastating psychotic episode. Like most of us, I had been through a lot in those twenty-seven years, and yet nothing compared to that time in my life. After my recovery, I was living a good life. I had created a thriving business and was in a very good place with my closest relationships. However, something was missing. What had started as a whisper in my heart had grown louder and louder, and now the whisper was a loud scream for freedom, for peace, for truth, for authenticity. It was a scream I could no longer ignore, and I knew right then that it was time to share my story and be free. What I did not know at the time was that by sharing my story, many more lives would find their freedom, their peace, their truth, and their authenticity. I was only the vehicle, for this message of hope was bigger than my own life and the ripples it would cause would reach people in all places.

It is interesting how the universe provides you with what you need exactly at the time you need it. It was within weeks that I had decided it was time to share my story that I saw a billboard on my way to work. Right there, in big bold letters, I read, "Wife, teacher, living with depression," next to a photo of a woman smiling. At the bottom it said, "Because mental illness is not always what you think," followed by, "Stop Stigma Sacramento.org." There it was. Without knowing anything about this organization, I knew immediately that this was exactly the one that would help me with my message. To say that I was terrified is an understatement. Up to that point, aside from my family, my husband and his family, and my closest friends, no one else knew my story. I had been told that I really did not want to share this because people's opinion and perception of who I am would change if they knew my past; but I just could not keep this inside any more.

Against the advice of my mother, I showed up for the orientation session of the Stop Stigma Sacramento Speakers Bureau with a draft of my story. I was told I would be asked to share it as part of the group activity after the orientation. It was the first time I had written what I was about to share, and it was the first time I have heard myself tell my story out loud to people I did not know. When it was my turn, I could barely get the first sentence out without crying and by the time I was done, I was sobbing. I felt completely vulnerable, scared, exposed, and somehow, ironically enough, I also felt free! Not only had I endured the moment, but those who listened to my story were also in tears and obviously moved by what I had shared. If I needed validation to know that this was a message more people needed to hear, I got that! That evening in October of 2015 would be the first of hundreds of times that I would share my story. I have never looked back. Now my mother is one of my biggest advocates and supporters, as are my father, my husband, and my children.

What had started as a desire to share this message so that I could live in my complete truth and feel free, quickly transformed into the need to share a message of hope, recovery, understanding and love. A message for all those who, like myself, live with a mental illness and do so in silence due to the stigma our society still holds as we struggle to do everything we can to live as normal a life as possible. Stigma, in case you did not know, is one of the top reasons why people with a mental illness do not seek help, causing many to continue to suffer in silence, self-medicate, become violent, lose families, become homeless, and in many cases, decide to end their life by their own hands because the pain is simply unbearable. How could this be? No one who is ill with cancer, diabetes, heart disease, or many other illnesses would avoid seeking help for fear of being stigmatized, but those with mental illness do so every day. The need to share a message of hope, recovery, and love once again transformed into something even bigger. This time it was bigger than I ever had imagined: this time it was purpose.

My purpose was to inform, educate, and motivate others to see mental illness as what it is: an illness of the mind. My purpose was to encourage, inspire, and guide others to seek the help they need despite their fears and, finally, my purpose was to shine a different light into mental illness and together illuminate the way for all those living in silence so that they can begin their walk out of the darkness, just as I did.

But one of the most important things I learned through my experience is that no one can do it alone. It can be a very dark and long road for many and providing understanding, love, hope, and support are not only necessary, but critical to the long-lasting recovery of those who live with a mental illness. I know that as human beings, we fear what we do not understand, and mental illness is still completely misunderstood by many. In many cases it is easier to ignore and continue to pretend that nothing is wrong rather than speaking up or seeking help because of what "they may find out".

This is why my purpose now is to ensure that people truly understand what a person with a mental illness goes through every single day; that they know the fight we fight every day we wake up just to function like a normal person; that they realize that there are more mentally ill people in the world not just living, but thriving despite their illness; that this is a secret most families share and yet very few admit, discuss or share openly with others; that not one person that knew me would have ever been able to say that I was mentally ill and none of them believed me once I shared that I was; that truly, mental illness is not always what we think; and finally, that just like you, most of us are working extremely hard to make a living, raise our children, find peace, be productive members of society, and be the best we can.

I have spoken now hundreds of times in front of groups, organizations, middle school, high school and college students, US Army Corps of Engineers, government agencies, and have made appearances on TV and radio shows. Every single time, someone always reaches out to me after I am done to share their own story with me. Every time it is either themselves, a family member, or friend who is mentally ill and who, like many, find themselves not really knowing who to turn to or who to talk to. The mere fact that someone else is sharing what it is like to thrive while being mentally ill is enough to create hope for them and their families. To paint a picture that ALL mentally ill people will be able to thrive and have a happy and successful life would not only be irresponsible, but also a huge lie. However, just as huge of a lie is the assumption that all mentally ill are homeless, drug users, unstable, unpredictable, irresponsible, criminals, suicidal, and so many more "labels" society has adopted for us.

As a society, we have made great progress in many areas. Unfortunately, we have lived in the dark long enough when it comes to mental illness. We not only need but we MUST, together, SHINE A DIFFERENT LIGHT into the lives of those who are mentally ill and, together, create the space where people like me feel safe, loved, understood, and supported. It is time to begin a movement to end the stigma on mental illness. It is time to write a new story and it is time to ILLUMINATE the way for those who are seeking a brighter tomorrow because they cannot do it alone. Would you join me on this movement today?

ABOUT CLAUDIA FERNANDEZ-NIEDZIELSKI

From an early age, Claudia became obsessed with positive information and positive quotes after her father introduced her and her brothers to books that would inspire and motivate them to always strive to be better.

Who would have known that the messages in these books would become her life jacket in dark times and also the light that would eventually guide her to find her true passion? Claudia mentors and inspires others to live life to the fullest. This passion led her to cross paths with one of the Masters of Transformation, Mr. Jack Canfield. Through his work she was able to completely transform her life by implementing his teachings.

Claudia is a woman who has survived and thrived despite the many challenges she has faced, starting with her diagnosis of Bipolar Disorder at the age of twenty-two. She lives with passion and is full of compassion for others, and she guides them to find their own meaning and re-discover their self-worth.

To learn more about Claudia Fernandez-Niedzielski, you can visit her website at:

www.ClaudiaImpactsLives.com

To book Claudia as a speaker or work with her as your coach, please contact her directly at:

ClaudiaImpactsLives@gmail.com

(916) 248-3004 Direct

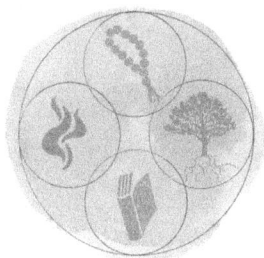

ROOTED

Angela Germano

'm officially a writer and have a beach house. Palm trees, yuccas, bay waves, and breeze, with the song of the seagulls waking me up from my dream-come-true. Breathing in the sweet salty air, I am so appreciative that the rhythm of my life has brought me to this moment. But how did I get here, to this point? The story is not pretty. I wish I could say it was from the love of my nurturing family, but I can't. I wish I could say it was my friends growing up that saved the day, but I can't. I wish I could say that I mapped out every milestone of my life and worked arduously to get to my dream-come-true, but I can't. There was no Prince Charming coming to my rescue.

I grew up in a not so great town where, even if I Google it now, I am not sure anything positive will come up. Let's see ... well, Trip Advisor comes up blank—I guess no one is planning a trip there. According to Data USA, 12% live in poverty, the average age is forty, and the median household income is $53,000 and declining. So, there you have it, not much has changed. Seems that many of the folks I grew up with are still there.

Sadly, my mom "never worked a day" in her short life, and my dad seemed to work every day in his life. From what I was told, they were a storybook couple. My mom told me that she was from a strict family, she had to make her own clothes and focus on cleaning and had one friend. She was not allowed to drive a car or have a job, other than babysitting. My grandmother vehemently disagreed with this, but she followed her husband's commands and never wanted to upset him. She would greet my grandfather with his favorite cocktail and dinner every night like a 'good' wife, and she told me that, deep down, she loathed every second of it. She had three adult children at the time and so much to say, but she held her tongue to obey his wishes. As a child I just took all of this in.

I know my mom loved her family and wished to obey and keep the peace, but she apparently couldn't maintain that when my dad came around. I remember the story ... a neighborhood boy, a bit older, joined the army and they became the best of pen pals. His nickname for her was Shotsy, which he believed to mean "lover" in German. When he came home one weekend, they solidified that nickname and I was in the works. It was a shotgun wedding for them, as beautiful as it could be for their young love, and it sent them venturing into adulthood, far away from my grandfather's strict guidance.

My dad had always been the rebel sort, making his own rules and doing what he wanted. I suppose he got that partially from his dad. My grandfather left his family's Catholic business to wed my grandmother, a Presbyterian. He left that comfort behind and my grandmother and he worked as a nurse and a baker to support their family of five. Hard work was a constant on my dad's side of the family, although I remember countless stories about my dad being in the proverbial doghouse for not following directions.

Getting to my story—forgive all my roots, they may be a bit tangled, but they get me where I am meant to be—I was born into heroic beginnings, with unlikely, whimsical, and mismatched parents gambling in the name of love. My obeying-with-every-breath mom and rule-breaker dad, who knew I'd turn out this way?

I look back on pictures and I was a happy little girl. I took becoming a big sister seriously. I was a dancer: ballet, tap, acrobatics, jazz, and pointe.

I was eager to learn and a conscientious student who loved art. But of course, the Polaroids don't show the government cheese, the abusive household and the cancer that took over our lives. No one wanted to see that reality, but my young eyes did.

I saw my dad's sorrow; I saw him picket. I watched him psyche himself up and hopefully fill out job applications. I admired his tenacity reading endless plumbing books, furnace repair manuals, studying auto mechanic magazines, all to fix the prized possessions we still had. I remember handing him a makeshift plastic bag of a raincoat as he rode a bike off to work odd jobs the next town over. He didn't make excuses, always worked hard and kept going, taking nothing for granted ... or at least it seemed.

When I was in fourth grade my mom was diagnosed with cancer. She had fallen at a party and complained about her back hurting. No one would have thought that this undiagnosed breast cancer had travelled to her back and around her spine, but it did. That's how it was explained to me. My mom was always perfectly composed, but I could see my dad's fear and physically felt his relentless frustration for the next five years. With all my mom was battling, she took on my dad's emotions as well. Life can be completely unfair, cruel, and uncontrollable. My mom's cancer came back with a vengeance, twice more. As my dad was in and out of our house, I scheduled doctor's appointments, transportation, attended chemotherapy treatments, gave my mom her needles (she had two IVs daily since her veins were shot over the years), tended to my five-years-younger sister and her education, as well as took care of our household. No friends were allowed over. Who would want to see the horror behind this straight-A, smiling dancer as I hustled through elementary and middle school? Mom held on as long as she could, I know this. She always prayed for life a little bit longer, voicing her goal, "I just want to make it long enough to see you walk through that archway in your cap and gown, Angela." My mom suffered a stroke or two in between, and, finally, after five years in our dreadful home, she passed away. I was beginning my ninth-grade year.

My father and little sister started over and moved five hours away. Neither set of grandparents, nor aunts or uncles, wanted me to live with them. After some time, my next-door neighbor took me in and cared for me during my senior year of high school.

I was tormented growing up. Heck, I was pushed into turmoil and then held under water, barely able to catch a breath. But being given an opportunity to join another household was pretty awesome. I witnessed how some took that home and those parents for granted, and I vowed never to do that, to anyone or any home. To this day, I hold true to that and I have no tolerance for anyone taking any person, place, or thing for granted.

My past was just that, my past. But I rooted from that tumult, I learned that I can control myself and I vowed to nurture and love me beyond what words can describe. I learned to be wholeheartedly independent. I learned to see the value in everything—every moment of life, of every experience, of every opportunity. My being had been challenged immensely, at a very young age, for years. My soul will continue to be put through the wringer, but I can control my perception, my understanding. I give it the value—I can control my energy and how I choose to utilize it.

Along my journey, I allowed teachers and coaches to comfort me as well. I fondly remember so many of them. My math teachers taught me it was applaudable to respectfully challenge someone intellectually. I would sit in the front of the class and ask genuine questions because I wanted to readily apply the lessons. Although they seemed to get frustrated with all my questioning, I knew it was because they needed to think on their feet all while the little voice inside their head was probably saying, "How in the world is she going to use the Pythagorean Theorem, or Calculus?" I earned the Math Award Senior Night. Truth be told, I thought they disliked me, but they assured me, no way. I challenged them to be their best version of a teacher every day in class. So even though in my younger "home" life questioning authority was seen as a negative, it actually was a high-level skill that my instructors appreciated. And so, I saw challenges as a positive opportunity.

My coaches ensured I took on every opportunity. They encouraged me to run for leadership roles within not just my school but outside as well. This allowed me entry into scholarship competitions to help me pay for college. My coaches made sure that we competed on dozens of college campuses so I could get multiple tastes of a new life that could be mine. They made sure I knew that I deserved it. They pushed me to audition for acting and debate scholarships. I credit my debate coach for helping me discover my alma mater, Monmouth University. He actually set up a tournament there so I could explore the campus and I fell in love. The feeling was mutual because I was accepted and awarded multiple scholarships, as well as campus employment. That assistance, paired with the grants I earned from my high school community, allowed my dream of college to come true—a new life that I knew I deserved. I kept telling myself to believe in myself, that I could and would excel in this new life. And I owe that voice, my voice, all to my teachers. I made the choice to acknowledge and listen. But it wasn't just academic support they provided; it was socioemotional too.

I remember going through a bad break-up with my boyfriend of six years and knocking on my soccer coach's door, past midnight, two years after I had graduated. The non-judgmental comfort she supplied changed my life. It showed me that what you feel in your heart, you can show that. The love that you feel, just give it.

I continue to open the door just as my teacher did that night. See, I not only went to college, but I took advantage of every opportunity in each nook and cranny I noticed. Now that I had my dream-come-true college opportunity, I safe guarded it every bit of the way. I was in total control. I went to bed early, submitted my assignments promptly, stayed on the straight and narrow and was looking to study abroad and land internships as a first-year student.

I remember getting a phone call from the pay phone in our dorm hall. The knock at my door and a voice saying, "It's your dad on the payphone." Why was my dad calling me? Turned out he needed me.

As I was finally in my own space, under my own rules, he needed me. Just as my teachers had indirectly taught me, I took on the challenge respectfully and opened my dorm door and took the call. Being there for my dad made me a stronger person yet.

That summer, I lived with my dad and my sister. As my sister was clumsily navigating through her high school years, they both needed me, and it felt good to bond with my dad. In an odd way, I became his teacher, guiding him to a healthier life, which I took great pride in. I shared my goal to start working within the Communication field. As luck would have it, there was a radio station within walking distance from his house and he encouraged me to introduce myself. I took his tip and it worked out. I became a radio DJ, news reporter, and even got paid for some of my news reports from The Associated Press. This was HUGE for me. Another dream was coming true, all because I made the choice to take that call from my dad, because I made the choice to open my heart—all because I had learned from my teachers to seek out each opportunity to make my dreams come true.

I didn't stop. I continued to stay focused on my new life. I went on to study Theatre at Thames Valley University in London and worked as a hair model and Pizza Hut taste tester to have a richer experience abroad. Upon returning to Monmouth, in only my second year, I joined the Forensics and Debate team and continued to travel and experience more than just my college campus. Once again, my teachers and coaches believed in me and pushed me to excel. They'd often dig for deeper meaning in my responses causing me to do the same, to make sure I was staying true to me, and following my intellectual curiosity. I was rooted in myself, living for me and believing in me, even when my beliefs and desires were different.

I went on to be a part of The Washington Center, one of the most reputable and sought-after academic seminars and paid internship experiences in Communications. Once I was accepted into this program, companies actually competed to employ me, and I got to choose. It was an amazing experience—being wanted. My own family didn't want me after my mom died, but these strangers saw my merit and potential and wanted me.

I attended numerous congressional events and became a valuable member of the environmental and educational team at a DC Public Relations agency while taking a full college course load and studying Congressional Law at George Mason University. I not only graduated *magna cum laude* but was offered a job at the same firm in Irvine, California. This brilliant group of professionals believed in me, but they weren't the only ones. Monmouth University offered me a hefty scholarship to continue my studies and earn my Master's in Public and Corporate Communications. Education, with all of its open-hearted mentors along the way, had afforded me a new life, a better life, one I had control over, and I could not pass up an opportunity for more. But once again there was a choice, and it was mine to make with all of my open mind and heart.

Growing up was not easy, but it may not be for anyone. We all have our own unique set of challenges, from disadvantaged neighborhoods, stereotypes, untrustworthy friends, being abandoned, feeling isolated, unwanted—the list goes on and on, but I always had a choice. There's always a choice. That choice is golden. It may be the winding path to new opportunities. My teachers, my coaches, my professors, my counselors, they all inspired me to keep going. I danced to the beat of many of a different drum for sure. But it was always my choice. My challenge was to keep my eyes open, my heart open, and my mind open to all the guiding light offering illumination.

ABOUT ANGELA GERMANO

Angela Germano is now a middle school teacher by day, college professor at night and raising her two children the best she can with her supportive husband. She's been an award-winning debater, writer, actress, constitutional law student, world traveler, drive-time radio personality, but always a teacher and a coach devoted to positively impacting people's lives so they can achieve their dreams.

Angela was recognized by the State of New Jersey as the American Legion Educator of the Year, an honor achieved because her students and parents recognized her excellence in teaching as well as her dedication to community service and leadership activities inside and outside of the classroom. She won at the town level, advanced to the district and county level, then was proud to earn the title for the state.

Angela has served on the Monmouth University Board of Directors and Chair of the Nominating Committee. She is involved with multiple charities such as Ronald McDonald House, American Cancer Society, and UNICEF. She is noted as having a true teaching talent; putting students at ease, increasing their confidence and allowing them to learn for the long term. She focuses on embracing teaching as an opportunity to inspire leadership, giving voice and choice to students through knowledge, exemplars, and opportunity.

Angela is also an inspirational speaker highlighting the specific topics of overcoming adversity, building confidence and leadership.

To learn more, you can reach Angela Germano at angelagermanopositivity@gmail.com

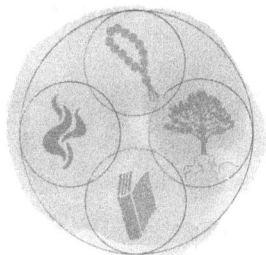

SNOWFLAKE IN THE SOUTH

Blair Hayse

When we are kids, we often dream of the day we grow up—the day we get married, have kids, a grown-up job doing something majorly important, and buy a beautiful home. I, like most other children, had the same white-picket-fence dream. I met the man of my dreams in the year 2001, got married after a few years, bought a home on the Tennessee River in 2006 and had our first baby a few short months after that. We had our baby girl the following year. My life was perfect. As perfect as one imagines it will be. I had the husband, check. I had the beautiful home, check. I had the kids, check. I remember going into 2008 with a lot of happiness. We spent a beautiful week in the mountains of Gatlinburg, Tennessee with the babies and my parents on a vacation that January, only to come home to celebrate our anniversary on February 23rd. I was the happiest I had been in life in a very long time. Things finally seemed to be falling into place.

When I woke up February 26th, 2008 it started as every day in my life did. I sent my husband off to work and got my two little ones ready to go spend the day with a dear friend of mine. Little did I know that this day would forever change everything. My life would fall apart in a matter of moments. As I was leaving my friend's house that evening, snowflakes started to fall. For us in the south, that is almost a holiday, because we rarely get snow. I was so excited that I could go home, watch it snow, and drink some hot chocolate. As I started down the road my cell phone rang. I could tell by the ring tone it was my husband. I dug through my purse and flipped open my phone. He asked where I was and, in his voice, I sensed something was majorly wrong. He asked me to turn around and take the kids back to my friend, pleading with me to come straight to the police station. When I asked him what was wrong, his only answer was, "Tell the truth." I dropped my two children off to my friend, assuring her I would call her as soon as I knew what was wrong and sped to the police station. Neither of us had been in trouble with the law, so my mind raced as I tried to figure out what could be wrong. I was taken into a room and interrogated for hours. After the interrogation I was informed my children would be removed from my care by DHS. They allowed them to stay with my friend that night and that gave me peace that at least I knew who was taking care of them. I packed their bags and took their stuff out to them. This was the last time my husband laid eyes on his children. I still remember him picking up our eighteen-month-old son and reading him a book before he went to bed. He held our six-month-old daughter and sang her a lullaby as she went to sleep. I remember walking to our car in the cold. I didn't know if the wetness on my cheeks was from the tears or the snowflakes that fell that evening.

I had no idea this was the end. This was the end of our life. The next few days were a flurry of attorney visits and getting DHS to allow my parents to have the children since we could not. In our marriage when things fell apart, my husband would always hug me and tell me it was going to be okay. He would make sure of it and tell me to let him worry about it instead of me. Somehow things always worked out. I trusted this time as he wrapped his arms around me and told me the same promise that once again, we would pull through the turbulence. As I looked over his shoulder, I saw police cars race into our driveway and within seconds he was being arrested in my kitchen. This was the last time I saw him free. What had begun as a tragedy turned into an unexpected loss, a door of grief that would never close.

What happened over the next months, I would never wish on any-one. It felt as if it was something you would watch on a movie screen, not something that happens in real life. I remember thinking it was a nightmare, hoping I woke up from it and realized it was all just a dream. Instead it was my new reality. I lost my life completely in a matter of days. I was so depressed I did not want to get up out of bed. I could not eat. I could not sleep. I could not even function. The house that once was filled with laughter, small feet running, and a happy family was now painfully silent. Every shadow in the house held a memory of brighter days that I did not want to be reminded of.

Loss is defined in ways we often do not realize. Most of the time, when people lose someone in their life, it is through death. They are surrounded by support and understanding of the grief they feel. They are allowed all the emotions they need because they just lost someone. There are support groups and fancy therapists. I lost someone too, but because of my unique situation it was not viewed with the same understanding, and there was a lot of whispering behind closed doors. I lost friends and people hushed me from talking about what happened. People told me to move on. There was not the same sympathy that comes with death. Uniquely so, there was no closure either. I had no grave to stand over, no absolute knowing that he was never coming back. Instead, it was a perpetual door of grief that would remain cracked for the rest of my life making it hard to move on and hard to gain closure.

In the process of all the emotions, I learned the importance of having a support circle that would be there. My family surrounded me as I fought through getting my children back. That took several months, but finally was achieved. I had friends who came and stayed beside me when I could not sleep at night and friends who brought me my favorite foods when I had not eaten in days. I had friends who collected money to help me through a time that was financially draining, and I had no idea how to pick up all the pieces that had been left shattered. I had friends who I could call in the middle of the night when I broke down crying and could not stop. My support circle has changed through the years, but I always have had a strong inner circle who knew my story and who was there when I needed a shoulder to cry on. Looking back, I could not have done it without them. In the present I am still blessed with people who love and support me when the waves of grief come in moments I least expect.

When tragedy like this strikes it never is contained to just one area of life. It has a way of making a ripple effect on everything in your life. My job was impacted, my family, my friends, my children, and on the list goes. Dealing with those waves can be hard in the middle of trying to process your own grief. You feel as if no one understands, or maybe they don't even care. All the anger, all the hurt, all the guilt, the list of emotions goes on and on. Mine turned to depression that I did not deal with, but instead buried beneath a life of working all the time. I advanced in my career and worked more hours than should be humanly allowed. I hardly slept. I hardly ate. My health started to crumble. I had stress seizures and a mini stroke by the age of thirty-one. I would not talk about my issues. I buried them deep, thinking they would just go away if I avoided them long enough. My son was struggling with his own grief. He had quit talking at eighteen months and regressed. He had anger issues and no matter who I took him to get help, he would not even try to talk. I was told it was his way of grieving. He had shut down because that is all he knew how to do. I was told to learn sign language because they were not sure he would ever speak again. I cried. I wanted so bad to take away the hurt. I was angry at my husband who I felt left us with all these broken pieces. I felt helpless that my children were hurting, and I could not fix it. I felt empty and lonely. I filed for a divorce and tried to cut off where the pain had originated, but nothing worked. I still hurt. I still felt the pain. I still grieved.

As with all major loss, there comes a time when one must face it.

One must deal with it even if it is the last thing they want to do. One must process the emotions in a healthier way. One never moves on, but we can move forward. After five years of insurmountable grief and burying it with work, alcohol, and a ton of medications the doctors had prescribed, it all fell apart. That day I woke up and knew I could no longer go on. I did not want to go on. I tried to take my life. I do not remember a lot about what happened, but I do remember the banging on my door, the paramedics telling me to stay with them, and waking up in a hospital bed with them asking me if I wanted to go into rehab. I desperately said yes. I knew that the time had come to face my grief. To no longer bury it. To find healing so that I could help my children do the same.

The week I spent in rehab was one of the best weeks of my life. I found answers on how to heal. I was forced to confront my emotions instead of burying them. I was taught techniques to use in processing my feelings. I remember one practice where they showed me how to set a picture of my husband up in a chair and tell him all the things I wanted to say. All the hurt, all the anger, all the sadness, all the blame, all the guilt. I could throw pillows at his picture and, in the end, rip it up and throw it away. Just to get all the emotions out was a relief I had never felt. A much-needed beginning to a long-awaited journey into healing. After that week in rehab an amazing bridge to healing began for me. I no longer sought the comfort of alcohol, I no longer needed twelve medications to keep away seizures, migraines, and ulcers. I no longer needed to bury myself in a work load that was inconceivable to the normal human. In this healing I found the ability to let go of certain emotions, face others, and to help my children do the same. When I became stronger in my healing, I saw them follow. Over the next few years I watched as my son, who had struggled for years to even talk, excelled in school enough to be taken out of delayed development. I saw a boy that I once could not stay in the same room with because of his anger grow much closer to me because he too began to heal.

The children and I began to heal together. We had talks about memories, we had talks about sadness, we would all hug each other in my big king-size bed while watching a movie and cry. We allowed the hurt to come. We also allowed the happiness. We began to make friends and to spend time doing things together. I was no longer working insane hours, so we could have movie nights, weekend getaways, and long trips to the beach. My children learned to talk to me, and I learned to talk to them. We realized we were healing together. The days of hurt and sadness grew more distant. They did not come as often. We could make it through holidays easier. We could listen to songs without crying the complete way through. It was not that I had forgotten. It was not that I had moved on. That would never happen. I had learned to move forward. I had learned to take one step at a time. I had learned that life would never be the same and I no longer had to try to mask the pain that came with that acknowledgement. I learned I could be happy again without being plagued with guilt.

Do I still have bad days? Hell yes. I still struggle sometimes when a song comes on the radio. I still see my children have accomplishments and am sad that their dad will never share those moments. I still struggle to handle certain conversations with my children when they are hurting. However, I am honest about my struggle. I use my story of healing and hope to help others. I remind myself daily to never forget the pain and the loss. I am remarried to a wonderful man who knows that my grief is there due to a huge love lost in a tragic way. I have a newborn son who I am now learning to raise with the help of his dad because I am used to being the only parent. I am relearning to trust in a relationship when I have a vast fear of loss. Grief is more than a grave. It is a loss. A profound loss from which you can never recover fully. It is true that grief is just love that has nowhere to go anymore. It can be felt in the deepest part of your being. There will be days you do not want to wake up. Days you do not want to go on. Days that bring sunshine and rain. Days that you cling to the rainbow in the sky because you want to believe there is hope and maybe a pot of gold. I can assure you that I am proof that there is hope. I am proof that there is healing. I am proof that the brightest candles have seen the darkest days. Keep the small flame of hope lit in you. Love yourself and others when you feel like there is no love around. Shine on my fellow brothers and sisters.

ABOUT BLAIR HAYSE

Blair Hayse was born and raised in Tupelo, Mississippi, and after graduating high school in 1999 she lived in Birmingham and Florence, Alabama before moving back to Itawamba County, Mississippi in 2008. She is an avid yoga lover, free spirit, lover of shopping, and mom to three beautiful children, Parker, Millie, and Jackson. She is currently residing in Mississippi with her husband, Jeremy, and enjoys traveling in her spare time.

Blair owns and publishes a digital magazine for spiritual entrepreneurs, *Live, Love, Light Magazine*. You can locate the magazine through Facebook @livelovelightmagazine and they always welcome new souls into their circle. Blair currently is a grief and loss coach, author, and speaker. She has founded a Facebook support group, "Life After Loss", for those who have experienced grief or loss to share and connect in a safe environment and find the support they need. She is passionate about helping those who have had loss in unique situations and helping them rebuild their life. She also offers free resources, a three-part video program, a six-week interactive group program, and private counseling for loss and grief.

To connect with Blair, visit
www.blairhayse.com
Facebook: @blairhayse

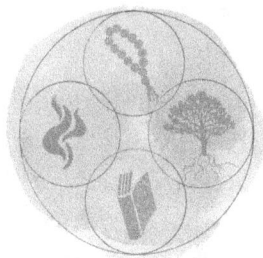

LOVE. LIVE. REPEAT.

Chloe Helms

What we see looking back at us during reflection goes much deeper than the surface. A mirror symbolizes our inner soul and what we project onto it is what we project onto society. Growing up, I struggled with body image and self-worth. From bullying, to personal loss, to struggles with mental health, I despised what the mirror showed me each day. It wasn't until my latter high school years that I was able to really pinpoint the root of my negative mindset and develop a means of overcoming it.

I was seventeen and sitting cross-legged on my bedroom floor, staring into a less than perfect, makeup-smudged mirror at the person I could not stand the sight of. I can remember listening to the dying clock on my wall ticking away the seconds as minutes and hours of pure thought and self-reflection passed. I spoke aloud to myself, words of love and hope, of who I was and could be—words that felt so foreign and false at the time. I told myself stories of how I got to be sitting there at that exact moment, contemplating how to turn my life into what I had always dreamed of.

One of the stories I recounted to myself was the loss of my grandfather to suicide. I was young, just seven at the time. It wasn't his death that affected me so much as the way I witnessed such tragedy affect my father and family. I didn't understand. I understood the actions that had taken place to get us there; however, I struggled with the "why." Why was this happening to us? Why did he feel that was his only option? Why? For years I looked at the effects that followed to be negative consequences to actions I had no control over. I pitied myself and my family and as I grew older and began struggling with a negative mindset stemming from separate incidents of bullying and mental illness, I took all of it and placed it into one large piece of baggage I felt I had to shoulder the burden of each and every day. Lugging that negativity around day in and day out would put me not only at odds with myself but with those I loved. I looked at them to provide me with happiness rather than providing it for myself, and it took me ten years to realize that.

That day in my room, as I repeated the words of love and kindness to myself until they no longer sounded like words, I chose to make a change. I chose to smile more and be aware of the good that surrounded me. I chose to wake up, look in the mirror and compliment myself. I chose to take the negative thoughts that inevitably entered and toss them away; they did not deserve a second thought and I would not allow them to control another day. I learned to choose, and through that I learned to love what I saw staring back at me in that reflection.

Forming a habit of positive choice is not easy and it took time. But if you tell yourself something enough, you'll believe it; trust me. We do not all have the same story, but as humans we all have our struggles, whatever they may be. Through this my biggest takeaway was realizing that the corny mantras and meditations I scoffed at growing up are real; they work, and a little self-love and positivity can go a long way.

Midway through college, now a different person than I had been three years prior, I started spending time in elementary level classrooms. I worked with children of all different backgrounds and ages but over time found a similarity that was unanimously shared across the board. Children, just as adults, want to be loved. We are not born with hate. It is something that is taught. And as someone who had aspirations to teach in a classroom of her very own, I would not have that play a role in the curriculum. I made an effort each day in the classrooms where I spent much of my time to spend at least a single moment with each child that involved one positive remark. As days and weeks progressed the kids began coming up to me with a positive thought or story each morning. They radiated confidence of who they were and wanted to be at just seven years old, the same age I was when I began struggling with my own self-worth. We even began choosing words of positivity, writing them on a small handheld mirror and having them repeat these words back to themselves; allowing them to connect their reflection with positive thoughts.

These classroom experiences along with my own are what led me to developing 2Lv, Inc. and where I am today. By choosing to look at what had happened to my family all those years ago and turn it into positive action, I feel as though, through pain, I have found purpose—a purpose that I hope can change a life as my own self-reflection changed mine.

2Lv, Inc. is a mental health awareness company I started at twenty-three years old. It stands for "to love" and "to live" because I believe that you truly cannot have one without the other; they go hand in hand. My mission is to educate individuals of all ages and backgrounds on self-love and understanding how to empower one's self in order to overcome struggles related to mental health. The company itself offers tools to aide in the process of healing and positive growth through self-reflection. My main products are my tee shirts. These tee shirts are tools to help provoke positive thoughts of self-worth and build confidence in the individual wearing it. Each tee shirt has its own unique phrase that is reversed on the front of the shirt so that in order to read it, the wearer must look in the mirror. By connecting the image of one's own reflection to a positive thought and consistently allowing those thoughts of positivity in, we can teach ourselves how to love what we see in the mirror.

Not only are these tee shirts intended to help in the self-development of the wearer, but each phrase is partnered with a specific nonprofit that focuses on mental health. With the purchase of a tee shirt, 10% goes back to one of those non-profits.

Whether it's passing by a store window on your way to work and catching a glimpse of the word "worthy," or having gone to sleep and waking up to brush your teeth to read the phrase "tougher than my troubles," or even a child preparing to start at a new school and looking for that small reminder that "their future is bright," these tee shirts serve a purpose. With the number of self-harm injuries and suicide growing each day at an alarming rate, it is time we choose to change our perception; and that starts with how we see ourselves.

To think that an idea that resulted from a night of staring in the mirror as a teenager is now a real product to help others going through similar situations is absolutely incredible. My hope for the future is to expand into a company that provides tools to individuals globally who are suffering. Poor mental health is not only a national issue, but a global one and it starts with providing an outlet and education. Although I am just twenty-four years old, over the course of my life I feel as though I have learned more about who I am than most at my age. In finding this personal understanding, I have been able to grow leaps and bounds towards a future that is nothing short of a happy one. Through learning to love the individual you are, you can learn to live your best life. Self-reflect. Love. Live. Repeat.

ABOUT CHLOE HELMS

After personal struggles with bullying, loss, and mental health, Chloe Helms took her own journey of self-discovery and created what is now 2Lv, Inc. As a current art teacher and having spent many years prior in different classrooms at different grade levels, Chloe was able to see the true need for educating young children on loving themselves and positive thinking. Meaning "to love" and "to live," 2Lv provides tools for children, teens, and adults that aide in personal growth and development of a positive mindset through self-reflection. While still working part-time in the classroom, Chloe has managed to partner 2Lv, Inc with three non-profits and continues to make strides towards ending the stigma related to mental health.

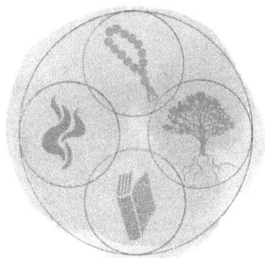

WORTHY FROM WITHIN

Penelope Jones

My earliest memories are of being very aware that I was the "pretty one" and my older sister was "the smart one". "Pretty" was always said with a tone of praise and "smart" was referred to as the consolation prize. My mother loved that as a little girl I always wanted to dress up fancy. She would set my hair in pins and rollers, prop me up in front of the bathroom mirror, and lavish me with compliments on being pretty, my eye color, having my father's olive skin that tanned so beautifully, and many other physical compliments. My father was in and out of my life. More out than in. He was a prominent, high-ranking law enforcement officer, well known to many in the community but barely known by me at all.

Almost every interaction with my father began with his commentary on how I looked. If I gained a few pounds he would say "Oh, putting on a little weight I see?" Of course, I would immediately lose that weight and he would say, "You lost weight? You look great!" My father also made it very clear that he liked my hair shorter. When I had my hair cut into a short wedge, he clearly loved it. If my hair grew past my shoulders, in a disapproving tone, he would ask if I was growing my hair longer. I treasured the brief moments here and there that I had with my father. I never wanted to say anything to make him feel guilty for not being more present in my life. I always made sure to look great, smile, laugh a lot, and be what he needed me to be. I actually mastered this skill with almost everyone in my young life. Be pretty, be thin, make everyone comfortable, and I would be loved.

This conditioning of physical perfectionism ran very deep in many of my family dynamics. I grew up in a female-dominated family. My grandmother, mother, and her twin sister were very powerful forces. I had a sister, two female cousins, and one lone male cousin. When one of my cousins got married, I was seventeen years old. I wore a very pretty black and white dress with heels to the wedding. Being that I am the youngest in the family, when everyone saw me looking so grown up and a bit sexy in my dress, there was lots of chatter about it. My grandmother called me over to her table. She asked me to lean in and she said, "See those sexy legs of yours? Well, they are mine. I gave them to you. You're welcome." I remember a family dinner with my mother, aunt, sister, and all of my cousins. The discussion was about who had the best breasts in the family. I was sixteen years old. I remember feeling down on myself that I never won this competition. Beauty and sex appeal were my position in my family. This is how I received the praise and attention that children need and crave growing up. The messages were many and very clear to me. My role was the cute one, the pretty one, the sexy one. Because I got very good at being those things, I also incorrectly believed I had very high self-esteem. I used to tell people that I was just born confident.

I married my high school sweetheart at twenty-one years old. Two children came quickly after. I gained quite a bit of weight during pregnancy and the second time around it did not come off as quickly. By the time our second child's first birthday rolled around our marriage was in serious trouble. By his second birthday we were divorced. This was many years ago and I have the utmost respect for my ex-husband. He is an incredible father and a kind and caring man. I married my current husband when my children were three and six years old. Almost twenty-two years later, I can say that the three of us had mastered the art of co-parenting before it was even a popular thing. However, back then, the circumstances of our divorce left me convinced that it was because I let myself go. I gained weight. I wasn't the thinnest or the prettiest anymore and here was the proof. Be pretty, be thin, be loved. If not, be divorced.

I dove into my role as wife and mother with a perfectionist mindset. My childhood was filled with instability. Both of my parents married other people only to get divorced again. I moved eleven times and attended six different schools. My children would be my proof that I was not my parents. They would have the life I never did. All the perfectionism and high standards I had for myself and my family were quite exhausting, to say the least. My third child was born and since my last child birth was followed quickly by divorce, this time I was determined to lose the baby weight. Diet pills, diet soda, coffee, chicken, and fruit were all I allowed myself. On our son's first birthday I weighed 115 pounds. Of course the praise and compliments rolled in. People really do worship beauty and being thin. Be pretty, be thin, be loved. Even though my husband was telling me every day he loved me and who I was as a person, I would not be convinced for many more years to come. I still secretly live in insecurity that if I let myself go, I will wind up divorced again.

My three children were in school and I was juggling all of their activities, working as the Artistic Color Director in a salon, traveling and teaching hair color for Redken, and volunteering in my community. Needless to say, I was doing ALL the things. Everyone was well cared for and had exactly what they needed, but I was so exhausted that I started to forget about one person along the way: me. We ate at the snack stands and drive-throughs most nights. I made fast, easy dinners out of boxes and filled bowls with sugary cereals in the mornings. Like most people during this time, I had no idea how much what we ate could affect our health. I was in survival mode and took the easiest route. If I gained any weight, I would follow the latest diet until the scale went down. Weight

Watchers, cookie diet, shakes, pills, bars, HCG diet with injections, not eating, soup diet; I didn't care as long as I didn't gain weight. During these years of abusing my body I developed an autoimmune disease called vitiligo. It presented as a patch of white skin on my right shin. On the legs my grandmother gave me that I loved to show off in shorts and skirts. The legs that got me a lot of attention through the years and made me feel good about myself. To say this was devastating to me would be a huge understatement. I know God was shaking me up, trying to get me to let go of my perfectionism, to let myself be loved for who I truly was as a person and maybe learn how to take care of myself better, but that is not what happened. It paralyzed me. I covered up. I hid. I had no idea that having an autoimmune disease was a huge deal to the quality of my health. Back then I just felt I lost control of myself. The control I worked so hard all of my life to have. Be pretty, be thin, be loved.

Shortly after this diagnosis and my devastation over it, my children began to enter the teenage years. The perfect control I had over them and their choices started to slip away, and I was definitely not equipped to handle it when the rough times came. A bottle of wine, pizza, and a bag of pretzels was my nightly friend. The mommy wine culture had started. I deserved it, didn't I? I was burnt out and stressed out. My weight crept up year after year as did my pants size. My insecurities were running crazy in my mind. I truly felt like everything was unraveling. One thing that never changed? My husband's love and desire for me. It shocked me, really. He loved me as a size four and he was still loving and wanting me as a size fourteen. But I was a very sad wife. It wasn't his fault, as much as he tried everything to make me happy, swoop in and problem solve with the kids, leave me love notes, buy me gifts, take over household tasks; he tried everything. But what I came to realize was, if your self-esteem is based solely on your appearance and how others perceive you, you actually have ZERO self-esteem. I've learned the hard way that it comes from within. I had so much love all around me, but I could not receive it. I didn't actually love myself like I had been pretending to.

During a particularly stressful time for our family, I was feeling so run down and ill that I went to the doctor. He walked in and said "So, how are you?" Immediately the floodgates opened, and I started crying. I told him some of the struggles going on. He mentioned my weight gain and said my blood work showed prediabetes. I was in shock. He pulled out his prescription pad and began writing me a script for prediabetes medicine. He also said he wanted to give me Xanax since I was so emotional. Something in me got mad! I thought, "Wait, I am in a rough patch here. I am not clinically depressed. Maybe I need to cry, scream, vent, work through this." What I did not need, and my family certainly didn't need, in my opinion, was me mentally numbed and not dealing. A flip was switched in my brain that day. I knew I needed to make changes.

I dove into everything I could find about health and nutrition. Lectures, webinars, books—I devoured them all. I started to make changes to my lifestyle and figured out how to cook more and eat better. The change in my weight, mood, and energy was quite noticeable. I found myself wanting to share nutrition and wellness advice with my salon clients. It was hard not to! They would come in talking about their own health and wellness struggles, and I knew I could help them—and help them I did! One client who was a breast cancer survivor implemented everything I shared with her and wound up losing 100 pounds. Some of my salon clients rid themselves of eczema, discovered food intolerances, shed excess weight, and gained major energy and confidence from what I shared with them. Now THIS was lighting my soul on fire! Not only was I helping them to feel beautiful on the outside, but I was making a positive impact on their lives! I needed to find a way to do more of this!

I enrolled in a holistic nutrition course and one year later I graduated as an Integrative Nutrition Health Coach. That year was truly life changing for me! I was immersed in personal development, exposed to concepts and ideas I never heard of, and I learned from the best in the nutrition and wellness world. When that year ended, I felt like I had finally started to figure out who I really was. Instead of trying to be who I thought I should be from old childhood conditioning, I started showing up in my most important relationships authentically. My already good marriage became so much deeper and more meaningful. He stood by me through all of these changes and no matter what I did, there he was cheering for me, believing in me. His love has been so very healing to my heart. Today the relationships I have with my now adult children are so honest, open, and real. I let them see me in my imperfections and failures and share my hopes and dreams with them. They truly know me, and I do them. Can you imagine what we all would have missed out on if I said yes to the Xanax and diabetes meds in the doctor's office that day? If I tried to keep my perfection persona up, if I did not finally see the precious gift I was given of working on myself, prioritizing my health, and really showing up for life, perhaps I would have robbed them of the love and trust that comes with honesty in relationships.

I love the work that I now do and it is very clear that all of my family dynamics, the conditioning I received, the struggles I faced were all preparing me to step into my purpose of helping others to take back control of their habits, choices, health, and to live their very best lives! Looking back at that girl I was, so focused on how others perceived her, not really knowing how to love and accept her flaws or her authentic self, I want to hug her and thank her for all she endured to bring me into this beautiful place I am now. I accept her exactly as she was and is now. I am so happy and grateful to find I truly am worthy from within.

ABOUT PENELOPE JONES

The journey that led Penelope to becoming a Certified Integrative Nutrition Health Coach began almost twenty-eight years ago when she entered the beauty industry. While behind the chair at a busy salon, she worked as part Artistic Color Director, part health advisor to her clientele.

After years of putting others before her—her children, her husband, her work—she was burned out. It was when Penelope was at her lowest, depressed and overweight, that she began to seek answers stemming from holistic nutrition. She learned to prioritize her health and she experienced astounding changes, not only physically but psychologically. Penelope has always been empathic and intuitive, so when she saw her salon clients were suffering in the same way she had been, she knew she had to help them. After implementing Penelope's health advice, they returned to her much lighter, both physically and mentally.

To formalize her training, Penelope attended the Institute for Integrative Nutrition and Holistic MBA. She proudly opened the doors to Penelope Jones Coaching six years ago, and to date she has helped hundreds of people gain energy, shed excess weight, and rediscover their best selves.

Penelope works 1:1 with clients and in highly successful, results-driven online group programs that run seasonally. To get in touch, email penelope@penelopejonescoaching.com

THE METAMORPHOSIS OF A VIRAGO

Janice Lichtenwaldt

Today, Virago is a derogatory term to demean "aggressive, abrasive, spiteful" women, but it wasn't always this way. In ancient Rome, women of high character who were commanding, courageous, wise, and morally just earned the title of Virago, putting her on equal footing to men.

***

His eyes narrowed, his face red with anger, invading my personal space just enough to let me know he was in charge. "You are so abrasive!" he screamed in the middle of the radio station while our coworkers watched on wide-eyed.

I don't remember my exact words, but I held my ground and stood by my decision. I was a twenty-four-year-old promotions manager at a new radio station. I'd been recruited for the role from another station and I felt my career was taking off ... and then this. I found myself in a very public argument with the sales manager. The topic? Which of our female DJs were "motherly" enough to host a Mother's Day promotion. The DJ I had assigned to host the promotion wasn't matronly enough in his eyes.

This was the first time I distinctly remember being called abrasive. For the record, according to the Oxford Dictionary, abrasive is defined as "showing little concern for the feelings of others; harsh". I was being called out not for something I'd done wrong, but rather because of something I was. While I felt justified in standing up for our female staff, this specific incident revealed a serious personality flaw. Where previously I'd been flying high with confidence, I now felt like wallowing in a gutter.

A question resonated in me: What should I do about it?

Ignore the criticisms? Move past the other incidents? Rein it in? Take it as feedback to be acted on?

Inexperienced as I was, I took the confrontation as legitimate, constructive criticism. I tried to play smaller. I tried to be compliant. While not always successful, I toned down my over-the-top qualities enough to eke out a successful career spanning radio promotion to tech start-ups to tech giants.

But the "excess" kept splattering out of my unrealistic façade like paint on a Jackson Pollock canvas.

Looking back I realized many of the exchanges over the course of my career happened because I was trying to play two people at the same time: one who was compliant and not "too much;" the other with strong opinions, who was, at times, fearless. Simultaneously, I was inelegantly setting boundaries without being fully aware or present of why. Setting boundaries is always a good idea. Being aware of setting boundaries, and being intentional, is key.

My lack of self-awareness got in the way. I still had a lot to learn.

As my career grew, so did my need to understand my impact on others. I purposely sought out ways to deepen my self-awareness. As luck would have it, a friend in HR was working toward 360 Reporting certification. A 360 report asks for anonymous feedback from your leaders, your peers, and those who work for you. I was nervous as hell to do the survey. Good God! What would people say about me? As I sat down to hear the results, my heart raced. I sweated enough to be relieved I wasn't wearing a silk blouse. The results? Awesome.

My superiors loved me.

My subordinates loved me.

But my peers? They only liked me. This crushed and confused me. Why didn't my peers love me? My HR friend shook her head and said something along the lines of, "These results are very high. You're doing a great job!" But I wanted to know why it wasn't the same across the board. What was I doing that brought my scores down only with my peers?

I took the uncomfortable step of reaching out to my peers to ask for direct feedback. If this sounds brave don't be fooled. I felt like vomiting before each meeting. Taking this step helped me learn I had fabulous colleagues who cared about me enough to give it to me straight: Bottom line—my peers thought I received too many opportunities.

I was always the kid in the classroom who raised their hand first and with feeling. For those who remember *Welcome Back Kotter*, I was Horshack. For the younger set: just call me Hermione.

My colleagues were right. I did get a lot of opportunities. Why? Because I took advantage of them when they presented themselves. I volunteered for stretch assignments. I campaigned for projects that offered opportunities to learn a new skill.

I was also aware the love needed to be spread around. When opportunities presented themselves, I looked up and down the line to see who else wanted it. If no one else stepped forward, I would. I'd be damned if I'd let an opportunity wither on the vine.

This perceived over-ambitiousness had made me slightly less popular with my colleagues. But I had their respect. Through all of this—the praise, the career growth¬—I continued to carry deep self-doubt. Doing what was good for my career was damaging my relationships with colleagues I cared about.

Concerned over the damage I was doing to my working relationships, I was inspired to form a women's group with others. The idea was to bring women together to build each other up, to share our stories, and support each other's ambitions.

Though I left that corporate job soon after the group was formed, a few months into a new position at another company, an opportunity to form a women's leadership group presented itself; I "Horshacked" it. I sent several emails to other employees who'd mentioned an interest. When the director of Diversity & Inclusion pulled us all together, she said we needed to elect a chairperson for our group. My first thought was, "Wow. What a responsibility. I wonder who will step up?" The silence in the room continued for a beat longer than was comfortable.

Finally, a woman at the end of the table leaned forward, pointed at me and said, "You sent all the emails. You should be the chair." Lots of nodding happened around the table. I said, "I'm not sure that's how you want to pick a leader," followed by my own nervous laughter.

The room voted and for two years I served as the Women's Leadership Network Chair.

Those first few months were hell. I didn't feel I had legitimately earned the position. I got it because I was the most "passionate" ... something that had burned me in the past. However, gradually, I settled into the role. Looking back, I realize my peers elected me because they were looking for someone who had the energy and drive to grow our new group. I am proud to say the group currently boasts a membership of over 10,000 women and allies.

Fast forward to my last years in Corporate America. I loved my job, loved my team, and loved the work we were doing.

During a professional development session, I asked my team to consider what they loved about their jobs. What brought them to work every day?

The day we planned to discuss their answers a voice inside said, "Why am I not asking myself this question?"

The answer: Developing my team. It was so clear. I continued the inquiry and wondered, "Why am I not doing this work full-time?" Then I thought, "Well ... that's laughable. Where could I do this full-time?

Who would pay for that?"

After I related my "epiphany" to a good friend in HR, she gave me the answer I couldn't voice myself. "Have you ever considered coaching?"

And the rest is history. I spent the next two years in training and certification. I planned to work another year, save money, then quit my job and open up my own coaching practice. I'll never know if I possessed the courage to quit the security of my job. The universe made the decision for me … and much earlier than I had anticipated.

Halfway through certification my position was eliminated. The upside was a large severance check staring me in the face saying, "Ok, lady, you said you wanted to do this. Now you have no excuse." I discussed it with my husband. Should I really try to start my own practice, or find another well-paying corporate gig?

He looked at me like I was crazy. "Of course you should. We'll make it work." Thank goodness for such a supportive partner.

With certification completed, I took the plunge and launched my practice. I was scared to death. Who was I to go out on my own? Who was I to offer help and support to others? Despite my past success the self-doubt, seeded so many years before, still clung just under the surface, threatening to shoot up and engulf me like dreaded bindweed.

Again, the universe provided the answer. Before losing my job, I had enrolled in a ten-month leadership course. I considered canceling. It was a lot of money to spend for a woman without a "real" job. However, I had committed. Something inside me said I needed to do this work. Don't chicken out.

The work I did over the course of this program, as well as the amazing people I had the honor to co-create with, revealed my true path. I discovered Virago. It was as if the skies opened up and rays of cosmic light shined down upon me.

THIS IS WHO I AM. I AM A VIRAGO!

I shook off the last vestiges of giving a shit about my big ass personality and embraced, with my whole heart, the perceived flaws that made me feel so small, so many years before. I made a commitment to myself: Everything I do from this point forward will be with full intent through the filter of Virago. It is a movement, a way of living, a way of being.

During the program all participants were challenged to create a personal leadership quest. My quest? To bring the powerful acceptance of Virago to a wider audience, and to once again claim it as a title of honor.

A quest and my platform were born.

After much thought, I decided a podcast was the perfect way to combine my leadership skills and big personality to reviving the message of Virago. The "I Am Virago" podcast provides a platform to highlight remarkable women doing amazing things in the world ... imperfectly. Imperfection was key. Our social-media-imbued-world paints an impossible, airbrushed picture of perfection. This is not reality. We must stop wasting time on diminishing ideas of flawlessness. We all have flaws, and those flaws make us magnificent. Our flaws can create our future when we embrace them.

I don't want the message of Virago to stop with a podcast, though. My dream is to create a collaborative community of fierce Viragos and allies by building a Virago Retreat Center near Forks, Washington on the beautiful Bogachiel River. People can gather in this sacred space, taking a break from technology and modern life to share their dreams and embrace their flaws. To learn, create, and grow. As part of the development of the site I hope to offer several weeks of free access to urban, low-income, and at-risk youth so they can experience nature first hand.

Will this all happen? Maybe. My path has been rather tangible to this point. I've succeeded at putting ideas into action. Nearly two years after taking the plunge, I have a successful coaching practice. I help others deepen their self-awareness, embrace their blind spots with humor and humility, and discover what success looks like for them.

And so again, I find myself scared, worried whether I'm up to the task. What I do know is that throughout my journey others sustained me. Whether they provided constructive feedback, screamed in my face, or cheered me on, they are all a part of my tribe. Nobody does it alone.

Embracing and celebrating my flaws, rather than trying to fix them, is what created, and continues to mold my future.

I am fierce. I am passionate. I am too much. I am Virago.

And so are you.

ABOUT JANICE LICHTENWALDT

Janice Lichtenwaldt is a Certified Professional Co-Active Leadership Coach who champions individuals and organizations to explore emotional intelligence, deepened self-awareness, collaborative leadership, and authentic confidence in pursuit of taking action!

Prior to launching her coaching practice, Janice enjoyed a twenty-five-year career in the radio broadcast, tele-communications, e-commerce, and online lifestyle guide sectors. Her work centered on marketing communications, promotions, product development, business development, and developing strong teams.

She proudly co-founded women's leadership programs at both Expedia and T-Mobile and is especially motivated to support women in leadership roles. Janice holds a BA in Communications from the University of Washington and an MBA in Sustainable Business from the Pinchot Programs at Presidio Graduate School. Janice graduated from the Co-Active Training Institute's ten-month Co-Active Leadership Program in 2018.

Her next adventure is to build the Virago Retreat Center, a haven for community-based learning, exploration, and creativity surrounded by the natural beauty of the Olympic Peninsula.

Janice lives in Seattle with her husband, Kelly, and their fur baby, Tiberius. In her free time Janice hosts the "I Am Virago" podcast featuring amazing women making their way through the world, imperfectly.

Please visit www.iamvirago.com.

Podcast available on Apple Podcasts, Spotify, Google Play Music, and Stitcher

Instagram: iamvirago

Twitter: iamvirago

Facebook: iamvirago

Email: janice@iamvirago.com

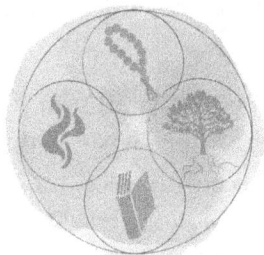

MYSTIC MOON

Fran Matteini

thought that looking up at the sky and seeing the moon was easy as breathing. But I realized I've never looked at it for years, didn't notice her presence.

The first time I looked up at the moon was actually a few years ago, when everything started to change, when I got clear on what was happening in my life ... I reached out to her and she answered.

What society has taught us to believe is that we are made of light and we come from light. We are taught that light will beat the darkness and that we will all be saved by it.

Religion believes in heaven and hell, in bad and good, in light and dark. Spiritual, evolved, conscious people don't.

Don't get me wrong, I'm not here to judge anybody, but to tell you my truth about being blinded by the light.

What exactly does this mean?

It means that we are trapped into a vortex of knowledge that doesn't belong to human kind. We are so blinded and so convinced that the light is the only solution to our problems, that we lose focus on the real work that we have to do to ourselves in order to have a life filled with joy, passion, sex, health, and abundance.

It's called shadow work, and the moment you realize that we are made

147

of dark and light, everything will shift into a new awareness and a new level of consciousness that will help get you through the rough times.

The biggest mistake we could possibly make is believing that the light (inner and outer) is the most beautiful thing in the world. Many of us actually try to chase everything that looks brighter, like running in a tunnel and wanting to see the light at all costs. But we need to accept the darkness around us and within us in order to heal.

When we learn how to work with both sides, everything will feel balanced. At the end of the day, if we constantly try to avoid the work with our shadow-self, whenever the latter arrives into our lives, we are not able to manage it, causing an emotional state of mind, such as depression, that could lead us towards suffering.

That's what the moon cycle is for. Because of the moon cycle, we are able to get clear directions, each and every single day on how to live our lives to the fullest, with the greatest fulfillment.

Following the moon cycle is not just about being happy every day. It doesn't mean that we are going to be productive every day. It means so much more. It means following a few single rules that we can apply on a daily basis in order to change our routines.

Some days are just about relaxing, some days are about being more sensual, some of them are about self-love, and some of them are for working.

It is such a rewarding feeling when we achieve something great during the day. It is magical to feel the way we are supposed to feel on that particular day, honoring the person that we are, accepting with grace what we are here on this earth for.

There's no better feeling than waking up in the morning and feeling great about ourselves, ready to do everything that we want to accomplish to respect our highest selves.

How worthy and amazing is following the moon cycle, accepting whatever comes for us, whatever feels good and having that balanced feeling running through our veins.

When I started to follow the moon's precious advice, everything shifted for me. I remember when I opened up my first solo circle, connecting with mother nature and the goddess. It was a full moon night, the candles were lit up, my soft cushion was on the floor, my witchy tools gathered in the middle of the circle, and my heart was full of fears and love at the same time.

I was going to jump into the unknown, I was going to destroy all of my beliefs, by sitting on the floor and connecting with something more powerful than me.

I remember starting to chant along with a song called *Litha* by Lisa Thiel, an amazing pagan artist that helped me get in the right mood. (The same one I'm listening to right now, while writing this chapter. By the way I'm literally having goose bumps, I feel like I'm travelling through space and time, and back to that moment.)

The moon was reflecting through the window and was illuminating me and the crystal bowl I put outside, filled with water and my crystals, ready to be re-charged. The smell of the incense was filling up my nose with the strong scent of sandalwood and rose. What happened next was surprising.

I started meditating and suddenly I found myself in a trance state, where everything was lighter than it actually was in real life. I felt something was changing. I had the feeling that someone was actually there, joining me, in that sacred circle where I only allowed my emotions to be present.

Tears started to fall down my face while a big smile of relief appeared at the same time.

This was my first connection with the moon and her power, with the power of something greater than us. Whether you believe it or not, something is out there, a force that influences our lives constantly, whether you accept that as reality or not. The moon will always be there, influencing the seas and the nature, so why shouldn't we accept that?

Ask yourself this question more often, and then try once! It is unbelievable.

That was when I finally realized that I had been given powers, a gift, and I had to learn how to work with it.

And that's what I do now, that's my passion and I love to use this knowledge in service of other amazing women, waiting to find out about their own unique gifts and how to use them to create miracles. I love to help women, who are afraid to flourish as the great goddesses they are, embrace their true power and their infinite possibilities.

Helping these women has become my only true purpose, my life challenge, my mission and growth at the same time. Because if there is a great truth out there in the universe, it's that we are never allowed to stop learning, to give up on our willing to learn and share.

My story is not easy to tell. I had many years of depression. I've been struggling with a lot of patterns and the fact that I wasn't as accepting of myself as I should have been. I suffered loneliness, but then I found out that being by ourselves wasn't so bad. When I started accepting that, when I started to learn how to do that, everything was easier for me.

I used to be that person trying to be liked by everybody, so I ended up feeling disappointed, neglected, and abandoned. While learning how to honor myself, even during those lonely nights, when the moon is high in the sky, I also learned that I can build my own world, my own reality, and I can enjoy being with myself, loving who I am, taking care of my health, and taking care of my body and my soul. Meditating has helped me a lot and being surrounded by the right people and the ones who love you is all that matters.

We are so busy in this society trying to find people who accept us just the way we are. It's hard, but that is when the magic happens. As long as we recognize who we really are, then the right people, the right tribe will follow along. And that is all that matters.

Have you ever felt this way?

Have you ever thought that something needed to change in your life?

That a greater good is calling you and you need to respond?

If this is the case, then make sure to connect with your higher purpose. And what better way to do that than with the amazing force of the moon?

Trust me, now is the time.

Now is the time, sister, because there is no tomorrow without being present in the moment.

So, follow the moon cycle, be with yourself, love yourself, and reach for the stars.

Because you are one of them, one of the most precious things on this earth, and you deserve to treat yourself as the goddess of your own destiny. And when you have the right tools to help you along this path, through this journey you will be able to have the life of your dreams.

Manifest the life that you want, achieve all the goals you have written in your journals, take action, and let the moon help.

GUIDED JOURNALING
EXERCISES FOR EACH PHASE OF THE MOON

Journaling During the New Moon

The New Moon is all about new beginnings. Gather all your intentions and release them into the universe. Set your focus and awareness on positive and loving intentions. Take care of yourself. Create what you have been dreaming about.

Journal: Your dreams! Let it flow, do not be afraid!

Journaling During the Waxing Crescent

The Waxing Crescent is a time to refine your vision. Have confidence in your direction and don't let anything put you down. You can achieve anything. Because you are powerful.

Journal: Your strengths. Refine your visions, find your confidence.

Journaling During the First Quarter
The First Quarter Moon is all about taking action. When facing obstacles, take bold steps towards a positive change. Meditate on your intentions and give them the right importance.

Journal: Your anxieties, your fears, and your action plan to let them go. Honor your why!

Journaling During the Waxing Gibbous
The Waxing Gibbous is a time to trust that your intentions will have the results you deserve. Align your hopes with the universe as you build up momentum. Keep taking action.

Journal: Your hopes, start to plan your future as if it is already in front of you.

Journaling During the Full Moon
The Full Moon is in its strongest and most powerful phase. Have gratitude for all that you have received and learned. Release all that no longer serves you.

Give thanks for all the blessings, for the presence of the Universe.

Journal: Your gratitude. Honor the abundance that you have already received throughout the whole cycle.

Journaling During the Waning Gibbous
The Waning Gibbous is a time for reflection. Meditate on your intentions and give gratitude to the universe for all you have harvested. Celebrate all that you have received and share your knowledge with another person who is in need.

Journal: Your wisdom, and all the ways you are growing.

Journaling During the Third Quarter
The Third Quarter Moon is a time for letting go. Release the negative energy and bad habits that bind you and cause you harm. Give back to

the universe from a place of abundance.

Journal: All the negative energy you need to let go of. Replace the negativity with your ideas for giving back.

Journaling During the Waning Crescent

The Waning Crescent is a time for rest. Take a few moments to restore positive energy. Nurture yourself. Your work is now done, and you can move into the New Moon with an open heart.

Journal: Reflect on how far you have come. Journal all the ways you have learned over the past moons.

It won't be easy, and it won't always be joyful.

It's going to be ugly at times, but the reward will be a blessing in disguise.

So many things have happened to me; some of them were tremendously scary, some were absolutely beautiful. That's when I understood that I had to deal with them because from both of those experiences I learned that the most sacred way is to finally serve ourselves.

Thank you, moon.

ABOUT FRAN MATTEINI

Fran is a modern-day mystic, CEO of the Moonlight Media Agency. She combines her business knowledge with her inner powers to give online entrepreneurs the help they need to scale their online business.

She uses her innate gifts and expertise to help you find a clear and profitable path to your life goals. She practices astrology and works with the moon phases to assure that any steps you take in your everyday life are the most powerful they can be. She is an urban witch, astrology advisor, and moon phase expert who uses moon magic and astrology to advise her clients.

She is also a former Virtual Assistant, Online Marketing mentor and VA Coach and she has now opened her own online agency where she offers her services (online and offline with her exclusive retreat planning service in London).

www.moonlightmediaagency.com
www.franmatteini.com
fran@franmatteini.com

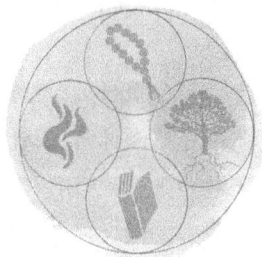

THE JOURNEY INWARD

Cheryl McBride

Everyone receives a tap on the shoulder in a different way. It's meant to gain your attention for someone or something. My tap came in the form of a sharp, stabbing pain, and it definitely caught my attention. That shoulder pain guided me on quite the journey that led me to connect with my inner self and deeper knowing, one that helped me quiet the external noises and listen to the whispers from within that I had tuned out for far too long. I leaned into innate wisdom and began to shift and move things internally.

I am the master of dealing with difficult emotions and stress, or so I thought. Stress has been in my world for quite a few years. The illusion was that I was dealing with it well. What I was actually doing was taking it on and packing it down, dealing with more, and then stuffing that down, until it manifested in my body. Finally, it said, no more! The pain I was experiencing manifested into a diagnosis of frozen shoulder. There is the traditional medical diagnosis of frozen shoulder, and there is a holistic diagnosis, which is what I know to be true. Once I researched frozen shoulder, I learned it is intense pain that can be the physical equivalent of a life coach steering you away from what doesn't support you in life. Our shoulders have everything to do with personal responsibility and our ability to carry out experiences in life with joy. If you feel you are constantly "shouldering burdens" or "carrying the weight of the world on your shoulders," you might experience a frozen shoulder, especially if you feel stuck in your current circumstances. Since our bodies are made of energy, pinpointing the origin of my pain and exploring my emotional and energetic patterns around what was happening in my life provided me with steps towards healing. Life certainly has a way of making you pay attention with intention. Just when I thought I was dealing with the stress and emotions that I had endured over many years, my body told me otherwise.

Divorce is a type of death. A part of you dies with the marriage. It turns you upside down and inside out. It makes you question everything you believed in and know to be true. It can cause unbelievable shame, embarrassment, fear, stress and dis-ease. I felt every one of these emotions and more as my first marriage ended in divorce. Honestly, my life initially unfolded exactly as I had planned. My first husband and I married in 1987 when I was twenty-two years old. We dated in high school, through his college years, and marriage came soon thereafter followed by three beautiful children, Patrick, Samantha, and Tori. When I was growing up, I wanted to get married, have the house with the white-picket-fence, and become a mom. That was my main goal … to have children and be a great mom. To this day, I still say my children are my greatest accomplishments. I was blessed to be a stay-at-home mom for many years. I was the room mom, the PTO mom, the soccer mom, and I volunteered for everything. I loved working on service and leadership projects in our community. I said "yes" to all of it.

When my children grew older, the whispers of my inner knowing began to appear and told me I was made to do more. I yearned to grow and explore beyond the only truth I had ever known. I wanted a part-time job and to go to college. I craved to know my own identity, and I could not stifle my desires. Those ideals were not part of my ex-husband's plans for me, and major problems and shifts in our marriage began to unfold. We entered into a very tumultuous time in our marriage, and for multiple reasons, among many things, we grew apart and our marriage did not survive. We separated and divorced in 2006. To say that it was an extremely strenuous time in my life would be a major understatement. I was thrust into being a single mom with three young children. I had no job, no college education, absolutely no idea how to run a household on my own, and I did not have my own source of income. The rug was completely pulled out from underneath me. Major feelings of utter incompetency surfaced. Fear and anxiety filled me on a daily basis. I constantly asked myself, "How do I do this?" In my gut, I knew the only way out was through it. I needed to stand up for myself, and that was only going to be accomplished by improving myself so I could create a better, brighter future for me and my children.

It came down to making the difficult decisions and following the path. There were definitely days that I did not think I would or could do it. I encountered many roadblocks and pitfalls along the way. It was exhausting! I cried endless buckets of tears because it was so freaking hard! Often, I would take life one week at a time, one day at a time, or even one minute at a time. Failing was not an option. I wanted a relationship with myself where I liked who I was. I wanted a relationship where my partner supported me and all my dreams, and I wanted to be a positive role model for my children! Despite the death of my marriage, I tuned in and really listened to my intuition as it gently nudged me forward. I learnt later in life that my divorce, although a HUGE setback, served as a comeback for me in discovering who I really was and what I wanted for myself in life …not Cheryl the wife, not Cheryl the mom, daughter, or friend, but Cheryl the individual.

I dug in and obtained my first job in fifteen years and began work as an administrative assistant at a local community college. I had a great skillset from all my volunteer work and that was the ticket in the door. I then had to prove to myself and my employer I was capable. Balancing being a single mom, working, and going through a divorce was no easy task. If it weren't for the support of my loving family, I would have never made it. I worked part-time for a year at the college and the environment was so motivating and inspirational that I followed those internal whispers and pursued my dream of a college education. I enrolled in classes for the first time in my life at forty-years-old. Oh, the negative self-talk I had to fight on a daily basis! I would constantly say, "Who do you think you are going to college now, and just how are you going to do all of this?" When I was on campus and going to class, I would think, "Everyone is going to say you are too old to be here, and there is no way I will make any new friends." I had to repetitively shut those voices down in order to forge ahead. I set goals along my educational process. Benchmarks were so important for me because there were many pitfalls and obstacles along the way.

I proudly received my Associate degree in two and a half years. I then gained full-time employment at the college and pursued my Bachelor's degree part-time. I finally began earning a decent salary so I could pay my bills. There was a delicate balance between handling all things on my own, and many times I wanted to give up, but I had my eye on the prize. If I had a dollar for every time I said, "I am so tired, I don't want to do this anymore," I would be a wealthy woman today. Honestly, who wants to research and write a paper when everyone else your age is out having fun? However, I stuck to my plan as I knew my ticket to a higher income and greater potential in life for myself was through education.

One of my biggest obstacles while in school was myself. Although I knew I had a goal, that didn't mean it was easy. My old programming was that I wasn't smart enough. I didn't believe I was college material. In my family growing up, I was the middle child. I was known to be the social one with the outgoing personality, definitely not the one with high IQ. I always thought the brains and good grades were left for my sister and brother. They were the two that excelled in high school and went directly to college. So, when I wrote papers for class and received A's or took a math test and passed unbelievably well, I truly surprised and shocked myself. Those papers got hung on the refrigerator. So, you can imagine how I felt when I graduated two and a half years later *summa cum laude* with my Bachelor's degree. The actual highlight of my academic career came years later in January 2017 when I received my Master's degree and graduated with a 4.0 GPA. I was nominated by my Department Chair to be the Student Speaker at my commencement where I addressed over 2500 people on the importance of living outside your comfort zone and not letting fear dictate your decisions in life. I have personally grown beyond my wildest dreams. Years ago, I never even imagined a college education was in my future. I would never be where I am today without the tenacity and perseverance I embodied. While we think life is happening to us, it's actually happening for us.

While I was pursuing my Bachelor's degree and settling into my life as a single mother, I began dating. We all know timing is everything in life, and to this day I believe my chance meeting of my second husband, Frank, was divine intervention. When you feel the hand of God on something, you just know it. Our relationship blossomed quickly and beautifully. Frank showed me how to love and trust again in a compassionate relationship, and I showed him unconditional love no matter the circumstances. He had never been married before and he did not have children of his own. My children grew to be important to him, and we formed a nice family. In March 2011, just a little over a year of dating, Frank and I received very devastating news concerning his health. He was diagnosed with Stage IV Colon cancer. We were both distraught and stunned by the news. Looking back on those initial moments, everything slowed down; my heart was beating so loud and fast that I could hear it thumping in my ears. It felt like someone had landed a large blow to my stomach and I had the breath knocked out of me. How could this be? I continually asked God, "Why? Why did you bring Frank and me together to tear us apart? Why does Frank have to have cancer?" Over the coming months, I became truly present to what really mattered in life. When it comes to your health, you never expect to hear the word "cancer." When entering into the unknown, it is very dark and scary. I felt so powerless as I couldn't control anything … not his diagnosis and not his outcome. It is such a myth when you think you have things under control in life. Once again, life caught my attention and said, "I am not done with you yet."

Frank and I discussed putting my education on hold while he was going through treatments, but he would not entertain the thought. Ever supportive and forever the optimist, he insisted I finish school no matter the circumstances, which is exactly what I did. The timing of his treatments fell in sync with my last two classes as I pushed it out to complete my degree. However, there was no big celebration. I did not walk in my commencement. We had other more important matters to focus on. Over the next year, we went to some of the top hospitals in the country and followed the best protocol to fight his cancer. We moved in together and we believed in our future. We planned our dream wedding in thirty days. On December 30, 2011, with 250 people as our witnesses, we were married. On that day, we celebrated all our joys, and we did not let cancer rule our outcome. Our total relationship lasted a short two and a half years, but it is indelible in my soul for life. Frank passed away on June 5, 2012 after his courageous battle with cancer. I was honored to be Frank's caregiver to the end. His last few days remain a blur and I am missing moments in my memory. I was blessed to be with him when he took his last breath. His suffering and pain ended, and I was in mourning.

I am not certain how I made it through that very dark and challenging time in my life. I quickly learned life keeps marching on even though I was stuck and feeling grief-stricken, angry, and devastated. My kids kept me going and became the main reason for getting out of bed every day. However, I merely operated on autopilot. I did the minimum to simply make it through each day. Sleep rarely came and my mind was consumed with racing thoughts. I was so riddled with guilt, thinking, "Why did Frank die, and I am still here? Was there something more we could have done to heal him?" I tried to establish a reference point of where to begin again. At this point, my internal dialogue was pretty loud. It was telling me that I bombed again. "Nice job, Cheryl, you failed twice." Married, check. Divorced, check. Re-married, check. Widowed, check. Check, check, check, and check … all things negative! I sought counseling to deal with my grief, stress, and negative self-talk. My counselor told me I needed an outlet. This is when I discovered yoga, which became my saving grace. To me, yoga is a form of meditation in motion. It not only helped me to reduce my stress and anxiety, but it aided me in creating a sense of courage and clarity and showed me the way to move forward once again.

Those summer months following Frank's death were arduous. I was learning to adapt to my "new normal" and working to create an internal shift, when, once again, another of life's setbacks struck, adding to my world's chaos. In October 2012 Hurricane Sandy hit the New Jersey shore, and Margate, NJ was my hometown. Hurricane Sandy was dubbed a "once in a lifetime storm." Residents were ordered to evacuate their homes. My daughter, Tori, and I left and could not return home for over a week. When we did, we were met with utter devastation. I could now check another box … homeless. Over a foot of water had entered my living space evidenced by the marks on the walls. I can still remember the stench of the bay water throughout my home and seeing many of my possessions destroyed. My spirit was literally broken. I asked God, "Why me again?" I couldn't endure anymore. I struggled to find a place to live. We needed to stay close in order to keep Tori in the same school system. It was difficult to find alternate housing because many homes sustained tremendous damage. Aside from the personal damage, many of Frank's personal belongings were ruined. That crushed me because I was not given the chance to let go of his things in my time, it was decided for me. Over the next seven months we moved several times, like nomads, living wherever we could and taking with us our salvaged possessions. It was late May 2013 when we joyously returned home amidst construction that continued well into the summer months.

There is no place like home!

My story doesn't end there. There is another chapter. It's a chapter of resilience and the pursuit of my hopes and dreams, of finding a new love and moving into another season of my life. I am currently living that chapter. Right now, it's filled with blank pages that I get to write. Sharing my story is an important part of my journey to fully healing, learning to let go, and moving on. Letting myself off the hook for all the things I did or didn't do or played a part in over the years. Recognizing what once was and is no longer, and what lies ahead can be bright and beautiful so long as I choose that each and every day. I need to consistently make that choice because I know I have only one shot at this thing called "LIFE." I hold steady to the belief that we should never stop growing, and all our dreams can come true if we have the courage to pursue them.

My meditation and yoga practice ground me. The teachings of these tools have transformed my life. They have anchored me in my personal journey of healing from past experiences, through love and loss, and through very tumultuous ordeals. They gave me courage to move forward when I didn't think I could. They taught me that I am the creator of my own reality and that I have everything within me to make shifts happen and it doesn't serve me to stay stuck. I spent many years angry with God because all that I lost and endured, and it chipped away at my soul. I needed to find a way back to Him and that has come through building my meditation practice. Meditation takes your mind from a constant state of chatter and turns it to silence. When all is silent, you release the external world and move to your internal self, allowing you to create a beautiful connection to your soul, to your heart's true desires, to your true self, and to your Higher Power. When all is silent, you can hear what your intuition is whispering to you and what your body is communicating. Meditation is a way of letting go and allowing yourself to simply be. I view my obstacles as the actual journey and the path itself. Although strenuous, they prodded me forward and guided me home to my truest self. My intrinsic grit is what helped me survive my journey, but my meditation practice has brought me to a place of grace.

ABOUT CHERYL MCBRIDE

After fifteen years of devoting her career to higher education, Cheryl felt the calling to follow her passion. She combined her love of academics with personal and spiritual growth and began her venture as a soul-preneur and founded Grit and Grace Meditation.

After facing several traumatic events, Cheryl found a sense of purpose through the practice of meditation and yoga. Their teachings served as an anchor and healing modality, creating a deep and radical shift physically, spiritually, and emotionally. This has inspired Cheryl to create a space for sharing what she has learned. Her goal is to encourage others to build a greater sense of inner peace and to help people live their best life, one breath at a time.

Cheryl resides in South Jersey and is happily engaged to her fiancé, Marc, who lovingly supports and encourages her every day to follow her dreams. She looks forward to creating many lasting memories as they plan their future together. In her free time, she loves spending time with her three grown children, Patrick, Samantha, and Tori, her dog, Quimby, traveling adventures, sunny beach days, dark chocolate, and delicious lattes.

Credentials: Master's Degree, Human Services, Bachelor's Degree, Human Resources, 200 Hour Registered Yoga Teacher , 200 Hour Certified Meditation & Mindfulness Instructor (Complete, Dec. 2019, Mindfulness Based Stress Reduction Practitioner, Certified Stand-Up Paddleboard Yoga Instructor

You can find her by visiting gritandgracemeditation.com or email her at gritandgracemeditation@gmail.com

Instagram @gritandgracemeditation

Facebook – Grit and Grace Meditation

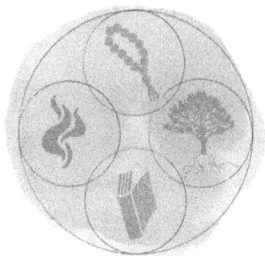

ILLUMINATED LIFE

Molly Peebles

" I'm on top of the world!" I shouted into the wind with arms raised to the heavens as I took in the extraordinary landscape that surrounded me. I was standing alone on the mountain pass between Mt. Salkantay and the Inca Trail in Peru. At 16,000 feet, the air is thin, the blue sky goes on forever, and the 20,000-foot peak of Salkantay rules the Vilcabamba mountain range.

The day before flying to Peru, I had taken my first solo flight in a Cessna 152. I had taken longer than most to get to that phase in learning to fly ... mostly because there was a part of me that didn't want to learn how to land. The part that loved being airborne, basking in the freedom of flight, taking in the bird's eye view ... that part of me resisted learning the finesse of the gentle landing. Eventually, I did learn, and I successfully soloed on May 18, 2001. I had achieved something I never imagined possible! And here I was, a few days later, having another adrenaline-inducing experience that recalibrated my understanding of myself and my capabilities.

I was traveling with a group of fellow Shamans, and we were descending down the mountain pass, through the deep valley to meet up with the final leg of the Inca Trail. Machu Picchu was our destination. Our days of hiking were concluded with Despacho ceremonies—gathering in a circle to offer prayers and gratitude to Pachamama, Mother Earth, for so generously supplying all that we needed for our human life journey.

The Shaman's Way, as I came to understand it through a decade of immersion, is a path of seeing the connectedness of all things and recognizing that everything has consciousness. The stones, the trees, the animals, the water, the earth—everything is alive and connected. Ultimately, we are all One. The people and events in our lives are our teachers. Nothing is by accident. Life is filled with opportunities to learn, to grow, to evolve, to awaken, and awakening into greater consciousness is the point of life.

When one is on a mountaintop, it is easy to live in the magic and wisdom of the Shaman's Way while surrounded by breathtaking beauty, far from the distractions of daily life responsibilities. I would find out just how hard it would be to hold onto the essence of the Shaman's path in the midst of "real" life.

At the age of thirty-four, I had three children under six and was a single parent. Life was busy and raising these amazing beings was all-consuming. The day-to-day life of being in service to them and their growth was my mission. We loved being in nature, and frolicking through the woods was where we all found our joy!

The carefree, spontaneous adventure of childhood gave way to the challenges of adolescence. Parenting teenagers is tough work! Growing up in Indiana and leading a sheltered life did not prepare me for the challenges that my children, coming of age in the 2010's, would face. The dark side of social media, technology, and access to any information through a Google search were just some of the challenges. Like so many families now, depression and anxiety came knocking at our door, and I was a single mom overwhelmed and working to keep my kids and myself afloat during a tumultuous time. I left my job to turn my full attention to my kids to help them navigate the perilous path through adolescence.

There was a period of years where I was in crisis mode and was tested to my core. I was trying to survive, holding my breath and hanging on to any thread of hope. I would close my eyes and go back to Salkantay and the thrill of standing solo on that mountain pass. I would breathe in that thin, refreshing air, feel the wind on my face and let the beauty of the expanse fill my heart. I trusted that there was a way through, and that the white-water rapids we were riding would give way to calm waters.

Life has its cycles, the rapids eventually subsided, and the nest began emptying as one ... then two ... of my little birds flew away to discover their adult life path, with the third close behind. My own life calmed and lightened. The storms had passed, and I came out of my inner realm to assess the damage.

January is the month of new beginnings, of taking stock of what is and setting a new course. I stepped on the bathroom scales and saw the impact of my self-neglect. I realized years of holding my breath had led me to weigh as much as I did when I was pregnant. During these years of inattention to myself, paralyzed with no energy for self-care, I had packed on fifty pounds without noticing. The stress of these years had left me feeling powerless and hyper-vigilant for the next crisis.

With a simpler and calmer home life—and a wake-up call—it was time to turn my attention back to the woman in the mirror. To reclaim my power. To be proactive, take care of myself and begin my journey of healing.

But where to start?! Having fifty pounds to shed, I decided I needed to take action and move. I started with short walks around the neighborhood, and those short trips started to get longer. I felt the return of some energy and I took the next step to join a gym. Two times a week for twenty minutes on the treadmill was where I started. I felt a little more energy—started feeling better. So, I walked a little more. By spring when the weather brightened, I was ready to set a goal—ninety miles in thirty days, an average of three miles a day. I posted my goal on Facebook and used updating my friends for accountability. Some days I did less than three miles, other days I did more to make up the difference, and I did it! I was on a roll now!

I discovered that when I was active and feeling energized, it was easier to turn down food that didn't serve my health, and the pounds started to drop. I was so grateful for the positive feedback loop. By the next January, I was ready to take my health to the next level and joined Orange Theory Fitness. Four to five times a week I was there, getting stronger, regaining my confidence, re-discovering self-esteem, feeling good about myself, my body, and my accomplishments.

Challenges give us opportunities for self-discovery and growth. After years of being handed hard challenges and the difficult life lessons that went along with them, I was excited to discover that by creating my OWN challenges through ambitious goal setting, I gained enormous personal power and confidence.

One day, I ran across a YouTube video of the Spartan Race, an obstacle course race that founder Joe DeSena created to help rip people off the couch and develop what he calls "obstacle immunity". By training for a race, doing it and reaching the finish line, people have the opportunity to overcome obstacles on the course that then become a metaphor for life. When you've scaled an eight-foot wall and crawled under barbed wire through the mud, you're better able to deal with a challenging day at the office. I was intrigued! Who would I need to become to go through such a race? I decided I wanted to meet that version of me.

A few days after my fiftieth birthday, I completed my first Spartan Sprint race with my son. Six months later, I completed another one, and I set my goal to complete the Spartan Trifecta the following year. The Spartan race comes in three lengths—short, medium and long. Complete all three in a calendar year, and you join the ranks of the Trifecta Tribe, which I did when I was fifty-one. Now at fifty-two, I'm taking on the challenge of training to summit Mt. Rainier, 14,411 feet in July 2020 with "Climb For Clean Air", a fundraiser for the American Lung Association.

With each new challenge, I reclaimed another piece of myself. Taking care of my body, I discovered, was the form of active self-care I needed to get back on my feet and move forward in my life. Taking back my power through action created the mind-body-soul connection I needed to heal and grow to my next level. I gained energy, clarity, confidence, self-awareness and self-esteem, and this path of setting challenges that improved my health and developed my mindset completely changed the trajectory of my life. No longer focused inwardly on my pain and exhaustion, I found that when I felt healthy, vibrant, energized and confident, I had a natural desire to turn my attention outward and be of service to the greater world.

This time of healing and reclamation took me back to my Shamanic roots which has taught me a path of self-discovery. It's been called different names: the Medicine Wheel, the Hero's Journey, the Cycle of Growth—I have come to know it as the Journey of the Illuminated Life. It is the path that I took to pull myself out of my depleted state and into the energized and expansive life that I now enjoy! It is a process of shedding light on what no longer is of service to us, letting it go to be able to stand a bit taller and to see a bigger perspective. By working this journey intentionally, it builds your resilience muscles so that when the unanticipated life challenge shows up, you are able to see it through from the place of cultivated inner strength.

Imagine the circle of a compass rose with the four directions marked. The Journey of the Illuminated Life begins in the East.

THE EAST

The East is the direction of the rising sun. It is the direction where possibilities lie. You stand on the top of the cliff and see the horizon, the big picture, the vastness of the landscape. It is from here that a vision of possibility emerges. What has been no longer fits. We feel out of congruence with who we feel called to be.

Sometimes, like in my experience, the East is the moment of realization that there must be another way, even if that way is not yet revealed.

Sometimes the East shows up as a big dream or aspiration that has been put off. At some point, the East will come and beckon us, entice us, to set a new course. Here, we are called to evolve, to awaken, to journey to the next level of expressing our authentic selves. It is the direction that leads us to live in a more conscious way.

When a vision is born here, it comes from a knowing that there is something better waiting. And it's exciting to feel at our fingertips a new way of being! A way that is more full of life, that will grow us, shift us, expand us … and if we find the courage within, we say "Yes" and cast a vision of a greater possibility for ourselves.

THE SOUTH

Once the vision is cast, and the heart has been hooked by the longing for a new way of being, we enter the South.

The South is not for the faint of heart, for this is where the work begins. This is the direction where we must confront what we must let go of in order to be the person required to fulfill our vision. This is where we confront our doubts, our fears, our limiting beliefs, our unexamined shadow. Like a snake shedding its skin, we go through the process of letting go that which no longer serves us. It is a time of emptying ourselves of assumptions we have made about ourselves, life and the world.

It is in the South that we let go of old habits. We may need to let go of food that doesn't nourish us, activities that do not uplift us, people in our lives that do not support us. The question is always, "Who do I need to become to be able to embody my vision?" The follow-up question is, "What do I need to let go of to allow that person to emerge?"

Letting go of the familiar way of living and thinking can be scary and leave us a little anxious. The solid footing we thought we had gives way to sand. It is here that we meet our resistance to change. We may say to ourselves, "What was I thinking?!"

But to go back to what was would mean to live in a limited way—and know it. And over time, that is soul-crushing. The only way to your vision is through the gauntlet of the South, to face the resistance and take the step forward anyway. And another step. And another. Momentum grows, new habits are built, and you cross the gauntlet into the West.

THE WEST

There comes a time when you reach the tipping point of letting go, and it's time to step into your power. It's the direction where the test—the opportunity—comes to step forward, to risk, to act out of the person you are becoming, not the person you've been. It is the direction that will develop your character, that will call you to dig deep and find the courage to no longer hide, to speak your truth—to live your truth.

This is the direction of stepping into your power by taking action. You run the 5K, you complete the Spartan Sprint, you start the new job, you go through labor and your baby is born and you become a parent, you give your speech, you say "yes" to the relationship, you join the club or the team or the choir. You step up.

The West is the direction of bravery and courage. In the South, you prepare, often quietly. No one but you necessarily knows of the inner changes that are taking place. But the West is about stepping out boldly in the world. People will take notice. People who know the old version of you may be uncomfortable with the new you. But this is your chance to draw on the self-esteem and personal power that you have cultivated, and boldly go forward.

You have the option to shrink back, to play small in order to make other people more comfortable but you would do this consciously, and going backward would come at a personal price.

Authentic, illuminated life is found here in the West when you choose to courageously embody your personal power.

THE NORTH

You cast your vision, you let go of what you needed to in order to move forward, you did things that scared you and that required you to act out of a higher version of yourself. From there, you step into the North.

The North is the direction of wisdom. You take stock of what you have learned about yourself, the world, life. You celebrate how far you've come!

You acknowledge those who have gone before you, your mentors, the shoulders upon which you stood to get to where you are now. You stand in gratitude for the people in your life who supported you in your journey, who cheered you on, who believed in you. You give thanks to God, your Higher Power, the Universe, whatever you call the source of your being for the opportunities for growth that brought you to the North.

Here, you stand tall, acknowledging the personal courage it took to get here. You look in the mirror and say, "Well done, you!" And you give yourself credit for doing the hard, personal work to set yourself free. You embrace this more enlightened, more conscious version of yourself. It is a time of celebration!

THE EAST

Once you've traveled around this circle and experienced the empowerment and aliveness that comes with following this path, you once again come to the East where the sun rises again. But you are a different person from the last time you stood on that cliff taking in the vast, beautiful landscape. When you come full circle on a spiral, you don't return to the place you started; rather, you are a few notches above. You have a different vantage point. And so it is with the Journey of the Illuminated Life. You stand on that cliff looking out on the vastness of possibilities with new eyes and with a different sense of personhood and purpose.

Who do I want to be now? What is the next vision I want to create? What new possibilities are out there for me?

You adjust your compass, set a new course, and begin your journey to the South to let go once more. You visit the West to step into your power, and venture to the North to bask in the new wisdom you have gained and to take stock of the person you have become.

This is the path—a spiral—of personal growth that will lead you out of stagnation and into the life that is your soul's calling and your destiny.

What would you like to change in your life? Where would you like to start? What is your East vision of possibility for yourself and your future? Every journey, no matter the distance, begins with a first step. It begins with a decision to move, to take action, to do something different than you've done before. It takes curiosity and courage. Follow a path that leads to discovering and expressing the deep richness and beauty that is you. The world needs your light! Now...take the first step.

ABOUT MOLLY PEEBLES

Molly has been using life experiences as an intentional path for self-discovery for decades. To work through divorce, she learned to fly a plane to gain self-esteem and break through limitations. After 9/11, she was the visionary and leader for Flight Across America, a national aviation event that brought thousands of pilots together to bring healing at the first anniversary in 2002. Molly has shared the stage with Neil Armstrong, piloted a replica of the Spirit of St. Louis, and got her first tail-dragger lesson in York, England. She climbed Mt. Salkantay in Peru to 16,000 ft, before there were hostels and a hiking path. She's been to Machu Picchu three times, took a motorized canoe up the Amazon to sleep in the jungle and studied with Peruvian Shamans for a decade.

As a Certified Success Coach, Certified Personal Trainer, Certified Spartan SGX Coach, adventurer and trailblazer, Molly helps women discover life meaning, inner strength and personal power through coaching, training, teaching, and outdoor adventures.

Learn more about her classes, retreats, and growth opportunities at www.mollypeebles.com.

Also find her on Facebook at Reinvent Your Life Now

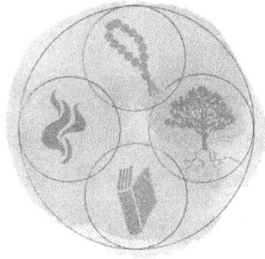

THE MAGIC OF SOBRIETY!

Tina Raffa-Walterscheid

November 24, 2004. I *thought* this was the worst night of my life; however it actually turned out to be a major turning point, a paradigm shift if you will. From the next day forward, I made one small decision that made epic changes in my life. I did not expect to make this decision, nor did I ever dream that one small choice would create a whirlwind of miracles for me just as it has for countless others! Quite frankly, on the night of November 24, 2004, I wanted to take my own life. The next day, on November 25, 2004, thanks to a very good friend I made a decision that saved my life. I had experienced suicidal ideation before, however this night was a bit more serious because I had a plan to carry it out. I went for a walk and set out to hang myself. I reached a point where I had lost everything that mattered to me. I lost my home, my family, and worst of all was losing custody of my own son. It was Thanksgiving night and my husband at the time was up north with my four-year-old son. I do not remember why he took him there, however being separated from my son on Thanksgiving was devastating to me. I had filed for divorce earlier and was battling severe depression.

I had extreme difficulty getting along with anyone, and I had moved in with my aunt and uncle. Being by myself was just too overwhelming. I could not seem to keep up with the normal everyday tasks of paying bills. I just did not want to be alone. It seemed as if everything in my life was a complete disaster. I could not feel any happiness and it seemed to me as if I was being betrayed at every turn. The more I tried to do well, the more misfortune always seemed to find me. I was going to therapy and I was prescribed several different types of anti-depressant medications, but nothing worked. Quite frankly, the medicine often did not work because I was not supposed to drink with the medication, but there was no way I was giving up my beer and margaritas. I was even told mixing the meds and alcohol could kill me, but I did not care. I continued to drink, thinking that it was not a big deal. I was barely hanging on to my career, was being docked in pay for calling in sick too frequently, and I was struggling to make ends meet.

I had no idea that the tiny little liquid in my glass every night was actually a vicious poison that would eventually kill me if I let it. I enjoyed "getting my drink on" and I had no idea that the cunning and baffling disease of alcoholism which runs in my family was slowly creeping up on me, devouring every ounce of self-worth and self-respect I had. When I suspected that I may have a problem, some of my family and friends would say, "That's ridiculous, you're not an alcoholic," and I would allow myself to be talked out of my tiny suspicion. Yet, when I screwed up, some of these same people were the same ones looking at me like, "What's wrong with you?" It is not their fault. It is up to me to find my own truth, and thankfully I did.

I had a tough time in the beginning admitting my alcoholism because I did not fit the characteristics that I thought defined an alcoholic. I thought that an alcoholic was the drunk on the street with a paper bag, homeless and dirty. Now I know that alcoholism strikes people from ALL walks of life. The alcoholic is not just the homeless guy on the corner with the paper bag. Alcoholism does not care how much money you have or what your profession you are in. Alcoholism strikes doctors, lawyers, teachers, and police officers just as much as the homeless man on the corner. It does not discriminate. The tough thing about alcoholism is that it's the only disease that will tell you that you don't have it. I know today that normal drinkers usually don't suspect that they might be an alcoholic. They do not even think twice about it. If you think you may have a problem, then I hate to tell you this, but you probably do. Normal drinkers have a couple drinks here and there, go to work, have healthy lives, healthy relationships, make good decisions, and don't run into problems associated with alcohol. Alcoholics make an abundant number of poor decisions usually resulting in damaged relationships, loss of careers or employment—the worst is that many succumb to suicide.

If you think you may have a problem, it is not your fault. Alcoholism is learned and it is hereditary. Alcoholism can strike anyone. One time I remember feeling really bad because I relapsed on alcohol. I was severely upset because I drank again after having eleven years of sobriety! I had achieved so much success in those eleven years that I thought I could drink again without consequence—wrong! Within nine months of that relapse I lost my home, my child, my marriage at the time, and even my vehicle was repossessed. It was crazy how quickly I learned that the disease picks up right where you left off no matter how long you stayed sober! The only cure for alcoholism in my experience is complete abstinence and a structured program of recovery that has depth and meaning. I had incredible difficulty forgiving myself for throwing away eleven years of sobriety. One of my sober friends lovingly said to me, "Put down the stick! No duh, you're an alcoholic. You have the disease of alcoholism." I just started over and I have been sober ever since.

Another important lesson I've learned is to "stop, start over" as soon as possible when I get off track with anything. It's human to make mistakes and the important thing is that we just get back on track as soon as possible. That term "put down the stick" really hit home with me. I was not aware that I was beating myself up so badly. I realize now that I am not sober because I want to be, I am sober because I need to be. I've heard it said that "sobriety is not for people that need it; it's for people that want it". I don't go to sobriety support groups because I think it's a fun thing to do. I go to sobriety support groups because I want to live today and I've learned that for a true alcoholic, as I am, that to drink again is to die. For me it is important to connect with my sobriety tribe on a regular basis otherwise I begin to think that I can drink again.

The disease of alcoholism is extremely cunning, baffling and powerful. We need our tribe to remind us of where we came from, and for me it's exactly where I belong. I can be around alcohol if I have a legitimate reason to be there. I have friends that drink. I have family that drink. I can go to places and events that serve alcohol. I just can't ingest it. The people that truly love and care about me do not treat me any differently. It does not matter what is in my glass for me to have fun and connect with others. I've learned from this disease that there is a little bit of good in the worst of us, and there is a little bit of bad in the best of us. Lesson learned is that no one is better than anyone else.

For anyone afflicted by alcoholism, there is some really great news! There is a cure for alcoholism, and I am forever grateful that I found it! It is now my mission in life to help others recover from alcoholism. My primary purpose is to be of service to God and to my fellows from here on out. Here is where the magic comes in! When I found sobriety, I learned what my core values were, and I learned how to gradually line up my life with those core values. I had spent so much of my life trying to please others and be what other people wanted me to be that I had no idea who I really was. In my alcoholism I had done so much lying and pretending that I could not find truth or meaning in anything. You see, when alcoholics drink (or use drugs of any sort) they often do acts or behave in ways that they would not normally do if they were sober. They subconsciously use alcohol (or drugs) to push down their conscious feelings. This begins an awful cycle of feeling awful about oneself then using more and more alcohol (or drugs) to push down those negative feelings.

The magic of sobriety is that I know who I am today, and I absolutely love the life I live. I am a proud mom, a good daughter, and a faithful wife. I am a reliable co-worker. I am an author, a speaker, and transformational trainer. I am an independent beauty consultant that teaches women how beautiful they are inside and out. I train others how to transform their lives into the lives they've always dreamed of. This is the life I have always dreamed of. I used to hide the real me for fear of being judged. I realize now the less I judge others the less I am judged. I've learned that it is actually none of my business what others think of me. It is only my business to be the best version of me that I can be and to help others do the same wherever I can.

The magic of Sobriety is that I know in my heart of hearts that my core values are motherhood, sobriety, family, honesty with myself and others, spirituality, and genuine friendships, just to name a few. If an activity does not line up with these then I do not do it. Sobriety, in a nutshell, eliminates confusion and loneliness. Now don't get me wrong, there is much more to sobriety than not drinking. This is where a sponsor or a coach comes in. All successful people I've met or read about all seem to have a sponsor, coach, or mentor. Before sobriety I always thought I had to do everything myself. I did not believe in asking anyone for anything. I was taught by a stepfather, who is no longer here, to be independent and he clearly told me "do not rely on anyone". He meant well, however I took this to the extreme and it did not serve me well. When I first got sober, my first assignment was to call my sponsor every day! This was a tall order for me as I did not want to do this at all. That phone weighed a thousand pounds. They were teaching me how to reach out, how to not go it alone and this was quite uncomfortable at first. The magic began as I began to work with a sponsor and take direction. The magic did not happen overnight, but it did happen! And sometimes in an instant!

My favorite magical moment was hearing my son say, "I love you, Mama," after several years of being separated from him. The biggest miracle by far on my sobriety journey is getting the privilege to reunite with my son again. Being a mother is my favorite role, and my son,

Luke, is my dearest treasure. Whether I get five minutes with him or five hours, I treasure every moment. He just turned eighteen and graduated high school last week. I have never been more proud of him and I have never been more grateful for the privilege to be his mom. He has taught me the power of prayer and the importance of respect. Loving our children is easy but respecting them and their wishes while still being true to ourselves is equally important. We can tell our children all day long that we love them, but I also learned that if they can't feel it, then it doesn't even matter to them. We must learn what our child's specific love language is in order to completely connect with them.

In the book *The Five Love Languages of Teenagers* I learned how to show my son that I love him in a way that he could receive it. Before I read this book, I was always trying to take him places and buy him things. From reading the above book I learned that my son's primary love language is quality time. I began inviting him over and just hanging with him at the house and our time was so much more meaningful. How awesome that I learned all he needed was my time and attention. This was not difficult because he is the most interesting person on the planet to me. I also learned a powerful lesson of the power of a proper hug. I learned that hugging someone for ten seconds or longer will emit a feel good hormone called oxytocin and bring you closer to that person. When Luke was young, I began to ask for ten second hugs and our relationship did indeed become closer.

Other miracles include repaired relationships, such as the one with my mother and father. There was a time when I did not speak to my mother for a few years! What a wonderful friendship I would have missed out on had I not had a sponsor to lead me through the steps of sobriety that ultimately led me to forgiveness and freedom. My mother and I have a love like no other and a bond that is uniquely ours. I would have missed out on that had I kept drinking and ignoring the resentments that I had built so diligently over the years growing up. You see, our parents did the best they could do with what they had. No matter what your parents did to you that you resent, no matter how evil or thoughtless you believe them to be, they did the best they could with the resources they had. Forgiveness is for you, not for them. Even if the relationship has ended, forgive them for your sake. Forgive everyone no matter what. Forgiveness is the key to ultimate freedom although often the most difficult pill to swallow.

I would not have found the magic of forgiveness myself without finding sobriety first. No matter who you are it never hurts to choose sobriety. I've seen countless miracles in my fifteen years of sobriety that I probably should write a whole book about. I've never regretted a day sober and neither will you.

If you would like work with me, contact me today to work your steps of sobriety and stay sober for good; learn the exact steps to reconnect with your child or reverse alienation, or discover how to feel beautiful inside and out every day! I look forward to hearing more about your sobriety journey and becoming friends as we trudge this road of happy destiny together.

ABOUT TINA RAFFA-WALTERSCHEID

Tina Raffa-Walterscheid is a #1 International Best-Selling Author, Transformational Trainer, Independent Beauty Consultant, Recovery Coach, and a Correctional Officer of nineteen years. She holds a Master's Degree in Business Administration, a Master's Degree in Clinical Counseling from the University of Phoenix, Arizona, and a Certificate in the Success Principles by Jack Canfield. She is fifteen years sober and is Founder of Raffa Enterprises and Single Parent Recovery Coaching, dedicated to assisting alienated parents and grandparents.

She was featured in the March 2019 issue of Recovery Today Magazine. Her specialties include recovery from drug addiction/alcoholism, suicide prevention, grief/loss, major depression/anxiety, and success coaching/mentoring. She enjoys speaking and teaching others to live their best life via the Success Principles, living the Law of Attraction, and sharing her own experience of strength and hope.

Tina is also dedicated to Animal Welfare/Animal Rights and educating the world about the benefits of veganism and plant-based living. She is a long-time member of Best Friends Animal Sanctuary in Kanab, Utah, the largest animal sanctuary in the world dedicated to making all shelters of the world "no kill" by the year 2025. To work with Tina, she can be reached via her website singleparentrecovery.com, RaffaEnterprises@yahoo.com, as well as Instagram, Facebook, YouTube, and Twitter. Her mailing address is PO Box 295 Norco, CA 92860.

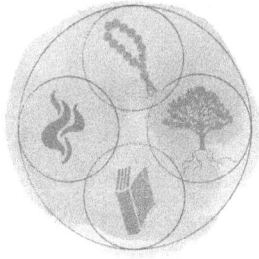

RISE UP

Chrisa Riviello

It's November 9, 2018. As I drive home from my group reading tonight, I reflect how truly blessed I am to be able to bring answers and comfort to this group of women. I am still amazed how I receive messages and answers to help guide them, and I love how it brings them a sense of peace, whether it is about themselves, family, or friends, those living and those who have passed away.

For many years, all the way into my adulthood, I truly did not live in the best environment, until I rose up out of that darkness. This darkness consumed every part of me without me even realizing it. I was given a lot of opportunities to learn big life lessons very early on. I was put into positions to overcome different levels of abuse throughout my childhood. From the reality I grew up in, to the marriage I ended up in, I had to rise up and see the light! And as of today, I am so happy I did. I am truly proud of the woman I have become!

HOW IT ALL BEGAN

Even though I never met my grandmother because she died before I was born, I know my gift is from her. My grandmother read tea leaves and the crystal ball. It was my mom's mother who did the tea leaf readings, so since my mom was familiar with this world, growing up in my house we had the occasional psychic party. I still remember my first palm reading at the age of nine. During that reading, she looked at my palm and told me how I would live to be at least 125 years old. Back then I didn't believe it, but today it is truly attainable.

My mom told me that when I was born, she was told to keep a cross under my bed to protect me. However, that never happened. When I was seven years old, I woke up in the middle of the night to see a woman floating in the full-length mirror in my room. At first, dazed and confused, I thought it was my sister with whom I shared a room, but I looked over at her bed and she was still sleeping in it. Of course then I screamed, though I was still so intrigued to realize she was actually floating in the mirror. I hated our basement. There was an old lady ghost that would hide under the stairs, so I had to jump two to three steps at a time as I ran up them so she could not touch me. When I was thirteen, my parents divorced, and life got complicated. Divorce is never easy, and I didn't want anyone to feel sorry for me. I kept everything to myself, though now looking back, I wish maybe I didn't so it wouldn't have taken me so long to understand life.

When I graduated from high school, I decided to pick a college that would get me as far away as I could be from New Jersey. I ended up in West Virginia. During my college years, I became very curious about psychics because I started to experience my own abilities. I would have conversations with people, and I would get feelings. I would know whether they were lying or being truthful. Also, I would know things about them without ever meeting or knowing them before. I was so curious to figure out what was happening to me. So, a few friends and I found local psychics in West Virginia to go to and get some answers.

After I graduated college this journey continued. I found a mentor in my hometown. She helped me for many years to develop my psychic ability. She taught me a lot about readings and intuition. It really was about trusting myself and letting the doubt go, but it took years. She taught me when I needed to feel safe and protected to surround myself with the white light. The white light would protect me. We got very close and she thought of me as her daughter. When it came to my wedding day, she was the one who helped me get ready.

My marriage began okay. The loss of my father-in-law had an impact wherein the dynamic totally changed—and not for the better. The best part of my marriage was giving birth to four beautiful souls. With each pregnancy, I know my abilities got stronger along with experiencing new ones. My ability to feel energy developed during this time. After my son was born, I had all of their astrology charts done. It was interesting to learn their charts are all interconnected. One time I was in the doctor's office with my third and fourth child for a sick visit. During the exam the doctor listened to the heartbeat of my daughter. Next, she listened to my son. She repeated listening to their hearts. She was stunned to learn that they both had the same heartbeat, which is unusual since everyone has a unique heart rhythm. They are all magical in their own way. They each have a unique gift. I realized I had to break patterns to save them because they saved me. So, in 2011, I decided to change my world for the better. It took me forty years to get to this place, though I knew it would be better. It was finally time to take charge and pave my new journey.

After my divorce, it opened up a whole new realm. I was receiving messages from loved ones that had passed away, something I had not yet experienced. In January 2013, I moved into a new home for new beginnings. After moving into my new home, I got a message that I needed to read more than just my family and friends. I had to trust myself and have faith to share my gift with others. I was to help those that needed my guidance and I was not allowed to charge for my sessions. I had to figure out how to do it. So, in April 2013, I created a Facebook page and called it "Mullica Hill Medium, intuitive psychic, bringing you love and light." And so it began.

All psychics read people differently. We have different gifts and abilities.

My sister is connected to angels for her messages and my other sister is an empath; she feels energy. I like to use the example that we are like hairdressers—it takes us a few times to find that right one that knows exactly how we like our hair done, and it is the same for readers. It took me a few times in my past to find the right psychic for me.

So, what is my psychic ability? At first, I was able to give answers to people and their questions whether or not they asked for them. I would be involved in a conversation and messages would just pop into my head. If I didn't tell someone a message it would repeat in my head until I told them. When I would tell them the messages, some were received, and others laughed at me. For example, I told a friend I saw heart problems with her husband. She laughed and said, "No, he is as healthy as a horse!" A year later he died from a massive heart attack. However, I have learned how to control my abilities, which means I can now turn it on and off. Just yesterday when I dropped my daughter off at her dance studio, I was talking to a friend who was experiencing discomfort in her abdomen area. I told her that I felt something was twisted or wrapped around in that area. She thought it had to do with the antibiotics she was taking for the second time, but I kept getting that message and that she needed an ultrasound. She texted me the next day after her appointment to say the doctor was amazed that I had that insight, and in fact she had scar tissue from a previous procedure that was wrapping itself around her intestine and causing pain.

Along this journey I have realized to put my faith wholeheartedly in trusting my intuition and the universe. I had to release all the fear and pain from my past. In the beginning it was scary, but it was something I knew I had to do. I have learned to forgive with the understanding that those who have abused me did not have the proper guidance. They had been misled down a path of darkness and that is all they knew.

I can answer questions about jobs, love, life, health, and relationships. During the reading I can feel any pain or ailments (if their back hurts, my back will hurt.) I can smell things, whether it is a favorite flower or cookies. I offer guidance; however, the end decision has to be my client's. I let them know what lies ahead but, ultimately, they have to choose their path. I am the messenger. I am here to guide them, but they must decide the path they will take. We have to create our destiny, but it helps knowing what the options are before you create it.

I have learned that I may not connect with everyone. I am not sure why this happens; it is complete silence, there are no messages, nothing. Also, I can feel when a person has their wall up and may not be open to receiving messages. One thing I have learned is to tell my clients everything, the good, bad, and ugly. I prefer to do face-to-face readings, though I can read via the phone. I love to look at my client and I can even look at pictures of people my client may have questions about. What I have learned over the years is that I am great with timelines. I once told a client during her reading in August to wait until December that year to make her move. The reading was so positive and inspirational, and she was so excited that she couldn't wait. She moved in September instead of December … needless to say, it had a different outcome and took her longer to reach her goal. I don't claim to be 100% but I do give myself a 98% accuracy rate.

I love what I do, I really do. I love the universe and the signs I receive. I cannot say it enough that living in a positive way and letting the universe provide is the way to go. I love that my kids live this way too. Do what makes you happy in life. Be happy, be positive and don't let anyone take that away from you. My kids and I always make our wishes every new moon, then we burn those wishes on the night of the full moon. We are amazed how with time those wishes do come true. I love being able to bring a sense of calm to my clients. It is such a great feeling when they tell me how much better they feel after spending that time together. One day I know I will have a place for people to come; I have already named it Harmony House—a positive environment to uplift and nurture souls. We learn that things are just things and what is important is loving yourself and sharing that love with your family and friends. So over all be happy and choose love, it has been instrumental in my personal growth and success.

Well, that is my story. One thing you should know is that scared little girl has been healed. She has turned into an empowered and intuitive woman, one who knows how to use her gift for the greater good!

ABOUT CHRISA RIVIELLO

Chrisa Riviello is a psychic medium with the compassion and talents to provide her clients with an exceptional experience that may very well change their lives. She is a precious woman with a divine soul. The pressures of life had crushed her, and she was beaten down badly. She thought it was the end. But, deep down, she did not realize that her struggles were only making her stronger. She picked herself up, rose above them, and showed what she was made of. She proved to herself and those that thought she couldn't make it. The struggles have made her wise and intelligent!

Chrisa has been on a spiritual journey for some time and seeking the gift of courage to accept her role. It has been amazing to be a true guardian to help others overcome obstacles and gain a sense of peace. She is honest, genuine, and truthful about who she is. She has risen up stronger than before and wants you to know, never underestimate yourself.

Chrisa lives in Mullica Hill, NJ with her four amazing children. Her favorite things in life are traveling, especially to Disney World, spending time with her family, and enjoying the beach.

Her website: www.mullicahillmedium.com
Facebook page: https://www.facebook.com/MullicaHillMedium/

I'M STILL STANDING

Virginia Rose

My name is Virginia Rose. I'm a published celebrity fashion photographer, an artist, a model, a dancer, and an actress. I currently hold two Board of Director positions for foundations, one supporting the arts and one supporting affordable housing. I started a wine company in Italy in 2017, and I own a fine art company, Virginia Rose Fine Art. I'm also a mother of three beautiful children. I have two lovely daughters and an incredible son. I recently started a Women's Empowerment Networking Group in 2018. There is so much to my story, but above all else I am a survivor. Being a survivor is the most important part of who I am. This story starts out a bit dark, but don't worry, she makes it in the end.

Let's start from the beginning. I was born in a small town in Florida. Both my father and mother were nineteen when I was born. My father suffered many traumas throughout his childhood, his mother's death being one of them. Instead of breaking the cycle, his pain was projected onto my mother, my brother, and me. It was a very difficult childhood. We were homeless when I was just one year old. I remember being at Grandma and Grandpa's house a lot after that, which was definitely a safe haven. We moved often because of my father not paying the bills or trying to dodge someone. This went on for years until, just two days before my tenth birthday, my parents got divorced. Was the reign of hell finally over? Oh no, it had only just begun. My father took us from our sweet mother and moved us to another state. We wouldn't find our way back for four years.

Within the first year of living with my father, I was moved to five different schools during the fifth grade. We lived in crap hotels and finally ended up settling in a matchbox-sized townhouse on a hill. That place would eventually hold horrific memories of physical and psychological abuse. A place where my body was in constant fight or flight mode, where I began to understand why children ran away. I was plotting an escape plan at just eleven years old. My brother was forced to live in a cold, wet, moldy basement. It was dark with not a single window. The cement floors were cold and stained. On Christmas day, we were given laundry soap and plastic molds and told to make our own soap. Does it get any lower than that? Because my bedroom was on the top floor, directly across from his room, my father could terrorize me at any moment. I feared he would kill me on a daily basis, until it got to the point that I almost wished he would, if only to end the suffering. I found an old pair of roller skates and I used to skate in the garage to pass the time while he was away, but those four years felt like a prison sentence. I was kept awake all night doing chores, even on school nights. I was bullied every single day at school and couldn't tell another living soul what I was enduring at home.

Finally, in February, two months before my fourteenth birthday, an idea dawned on me. I was getting my brother and myself out of there for good. Now keep in mind at this time there were no cellphones or internet—if a parent didn't want you talking to someone, you were off the grid. But I saw a commercial for 1-800-COLLECT. Wow, if I could get to a phone, even at the neighbor's house, I could call my grandparents to come rescue us! I waited a few days for the perfect opportunity. My next-door-neighbor, Joseph, was my brother's age. When his dad headed to work, I skipped school and asked Joseph to do the same. He let me use his phone to make a collect call and I called my grandmother. She and my grandfather drove from three states away, through the night, and came to rescue my brother and me. I have never been so happy to ride in the back of a Buick Roadmaster in all my life. Finally, I was headed to see my mother's sweet, smiling face. "Will she recognize me?" I thought to myself. I hadn't seen her in years. I wasn't a child anymore. Would we get a little house and a tiny dog and go to a nice school and live happily ever after? Well, that was my wish, but hardly the case.

Unfortunately, due to the trauma my mother suffered during the years we were separated, she had become severely depressed. She tried to care for us the best she knew how, but things were never how I pictured they would be once we were reunited. We lived in severe poverty in a dilapidated trailer—a steel box that would be yet another place of pain. My brother slowly became an addict. I started figure skating during this time, and it helped heal some of the traumas I had experienced. But I was the victim of rape, and by age sixteen, I had enough. I chose to move to Orlando, Florida with a friend and got a job at Disney World as a photographer, which would start the journey that led to where I am this very day.

Two years later, at age eighteen, I married. I wanted to start my own family. In my young mind I thought, somehow, if I could just have my own life, my own children, and my own home, I could rectify all the years of trauma I had suffered. I could rebuild. I wanted love more than anything on the planet. I wanted to create a world I actually wanted to live in. As much as I wanted the white-picket-fence, it always seemed out of my grasp. My relationship quickly turned into one filled with domestic violence, great sadness, and unimaginable pain. Through it all I never gave up. I brought three beautiful children into the world. I tried to protect them with all my might and teach them love, compassion, and empathy: the important things in this world.

My first child, Emily, was born with a rare kidney disorder when I was nineteen. At just nine-days-old, she suffered from a 104.7 fever and eventually coded and had to be resuscitated numerous times. We lived in hospitals for nearly four months, until she eventually had an exploratory surgery that saved her life but took months to recover from. It was the scariest thing I had ever seen. My tiny baby fought for her life on a daily basis. With no medical background I cared for her around the clock. She is definitely my miracle baby. She is sixteen now and I am so grateful for her every day.

Next came my daughter, Rachel, in 2004, the worst year for hurricanes in Florida up to that point. We moved into a new house the day she was born. Just three weeks after, we were hit by Hurricane Charlie, which left us without power for weeks. Next came Hurricane Francis, then Ivan, and lastly, Jeanne. She hit us twice. We lost our home and nearly everything in it. It was one of the darkest times in my life. I remember holding my tiny girl in the closet with her sister sleeping on the floor alongside us, praying the roof wouldn't blow off and the water wouldn't rush in while we sat in total darkness, listening to gusts of 145 mph winds and tornados destroying things in the not-so-far distance. I was twenty-one. I needed a break in life, just one.

That holiday season, with nowhere to go, we made our way up the east coast with only our car, a little money in our pocket, and the things we could fit in our Toyota. We finally stopped after two days of driving through a blizzard and ended up in Connecticut. I didn't know a single soul. I was starting over, yet again. Could this be real? I rented a small mother-in-law apartment from a distant relative and we called that place home for four months. I made the best of it. But what a time of reflection and loneliness. My family and I were now separated by nearly ten states and hundreds of miles. But I knew I had to make it on my own for the two precious daughters I had brought into the world.

Right before I got pregnant with my son, I suffered a painful miscarriage, so finding out I was pregnant with a healthy baby boy was such a blessing. Through much of my pregnancy I was afraid of losing him and almost did when I was about seven months pregnant. I collapsed at work but, thankfully, I was able to carry him to term and he was born healthy and happy at nearly nine pounds. So, now there were three. I had always wanted to be a mother, and though things were tough sometimes, my children were and are my world.

Now that I had three children to support, it was time to begin a plan of action. So many times, I wanted to give up. It would take me nearly fourteen years to find success, but every due I paid, every failure and triumph led to me to the exact path and plan that God had over my life. I stepped out in faith. I began to journal my ideas, hopes, and dreams for the future. Slowly, I put the pieces together. I had to overcome anxiety, depression, and PTSD in order to bring my dreams of becoming a successful photographer, artist, and so much more to life. It wasn't easy, but I never quit. If I could give another woman advice, that would be it: never quit. Easier said than done, I know. But you will thank yourself in the end.

Through all of these traumas and tragic events, I really had to learn how to be brave. I had to teach myself to follow my dreams. Give myself permission to fail and forgive myself when I did, then try again. I had to learn to be grateful for what was going right instead of the things that were going wrong. Through this journey I learned that I am stronger than I ever knew I could possibly be. My entire journey led me to exactly this moment: writing for this book, becoming an artist and using the pain for healing, putting myself out there and having empathy for others who have also had great suffering.

One of the most significant things I learned from all I have endured is that self-care is one of the most important things in the world. How can you be a good mother, artist, or entrepreneur when you don't take care of you? Practicing self-care saved my life. I learned to meditate and center my spirit. Exercising, painting, having lunch with a friend—doing things that fill your spirit are some of the most powerful healing tools you can imagine. I brought myself back and began healing day by day. There is so much more to my story, and I can't wait to see what the future holds.

Over the last two years I have formed some amazing healing, loving, supportive, and beautiful friendships with truly incredible women. I just want to say thank you for your wisdom. I couldn't have done it without you. I would like to leave you all with this quote a wise woman, Jena Garcia, once told me: "When we rise with the tides, we rise together." Someone can look very successful or beautiful, as if they have it all together. But you never know what someone has been through. So, go out in to the world. Follow your dreams no matter your past or what you have been through. Believe that you can create your own success, form long-lasting, respectful, and loving relationships with women. You will need them, I promise. And always take time to recharge your batteries, heal, love, and protect your spirit at all costs.

ABOUT VIRGINIA ROSE

Published hundreds of times all over the world in print and digital media, Virginia Rose is an internationally renowned fine art photographer, sought after for her incomparably beautiful and evocative theme shoots, modeling portfolios, book and album covers, and specialty photography.

Distinguished for her creative vision and technical expertise in a career that has spanned nearl two decades, Virginia began professionally as a celebrity and character photographer. She has continued to provide her singular photographic vision to star clients in music, stage, and screen, such as Nyle DiMarco, winner of America's Next Top Model and Dancing with the Stars.

Virginia is a fashion photographer, business woman, entrepreneuer, wine maker, model, actress and devoted mother of three. Virginia divides her time between raising her family, client work at her private exclusive studio in D.C., traveling to Italy to work on her wine company Virginia Rose vino and for fashion photo shoots. Her hobbies include painting, writing, swimming, and traveling as much as she can.

Virginia connects with the greater community as well as her clients. Grateful to God for her success, Virginia believes strongly in giving back, paying it forward by donating her time and talent to charity fundraisers and the children's theater in her community.

Virginia brings an unmistakable authenticity and integrity to her work, imbued with her joy and artistic passion. Whether it be a Virginia Rose Fine Art piece or a beautifully hand-crafted bottle of Virginia Rose Vino, you can count on it being distinctive and beautifully unique.

www.vrhphotography.com
www.virginiarosefineart.com
Facebook:Virginia Hodges
Instagram @vrfineart

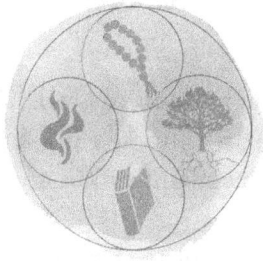

PEACE PREVAIL

Mandy Scanlon

nxiety is a word used very often in our society today. We live in a stressed-out world. Women, specifically, face a tremendous amount of stress. Many of us have many roles, like wife, mother, caretaker, homemaker, and professional. Just writing that could stress me out! Ha! I am not saying that men have less stress than us, but as women, we have a lot on our minds, like the grocery list, homework, running kids to events, cleaning, cooking, and taking care of sick kids. All while trying to keep ourselves somewhat together! I know some women who have had a nervous breakdown over all of this. I was really close to having one myself.

After years of infertility, my kids were still very young, and I started to become obsessive compulsive, germophobic, scared of something happening to me or my family, and downright depressed. It was the scariest time of my life. If you have ever experienced living in this fear, the negative talk in your head or the moment of a panic attack, then you know it feels like you are living in a scene from the movie Halloween! You feel scared to death, your heart races constantly, and you just want to run, but there is no where to go.

Anxiety caused panic attacks weekly, if not daily. It caused me to live with a constant stomachache. I could not eat much and the adrenaline that pumped through my body all day from the fear caused me to lose a lot of weight. I was pale, thin, and my hair was falling out, either from the stress or from the malnutrition my body was going through. I looked sick.

Although I knew it was not normal, I feared bringing my children anywhere there were going to be people because they could potentially get sick. I figured it would pass and I would get over it. Every day, in and out, I would think negative thoughts, building up the anxiety more and more. I would drive in the car, thinking how horrible it would be if they came down with something. I would think about how they would suffer, like when my daughter had hand, foot, and mouth virus. She cried for two days straight. I could never go through that again. This kind of thinking, whether it be about illness, or a job interview, will do nothing but bring you down. I clearly was in a horrible spiral downward, but did not see the future of panic attacks coming.

I remember my first panic attack. My heart was pounding, my hands were sweaty, and I felt dizzy and sick to my stomach. I thought I was getting a stomach bug, which was one of my biggest fears, so things progressed quickly with this attack. I threw up a couple times, while still shaking and sweating, and scary thoughts ran through my head. I was in a fog, like I was out of my body, and then my hands went numb. My freaking hands were numb! "That's it, I am dying." That is what I thought. "I'm dead." I yelled for my husband who was downstairs with our kids. He got me a cold rag as I sobbed that it was the end and I needed to go to the hospital. It seemed like this went on for an hour, but in actuality, it was probably only a few minutes. He sat with me and, somehow, I started to come out of the attack a bit. He went back downstairs with the kids and I called my mom. I told her I was sick with a stomach bug and that my hands went numb. After talking about the symptoms, she said, "I think you just had a panic attack." "What? No, I am sick," I said. She said, "Well, maybe, but I think it was a panic attack." I went to bed and didn't get sick again, but I felt like I ran a marathon, barefoot, in a blizzard. I was exhausted, my body ached, and I had chills. I went to work the next day but looked and felt horrible. A week later I had another one. For a few minutes I thought, "Ugh, I am sick again," but realized afterwards that I was having a panic attack.

I now feared having a panic attack, plus all of the other things. I eventually became so scared and depressed that I wasn't sure I wanted to live anymore. This was surely no way to live. My husband and kids saw me crying all of the time. I was cranky and tired because instead of sleeping, I would stay up all night thinking, "What if it happens again?" A few times when my husband got home from work, I would go for a ride in my car. I would think, "I should just go away, I am ruining their lives, they would be better off without me." Thank goodness, my love for myself was bigger than these thoughts.

I woke up one day and thought, "I cannot live like this! There has to be a way to get better." Mind you, I had been to a million doctors already, but I knew there was some other way to get better. I had been researching anxiety and depression online, but I truly did not understand it. I could not comprehend that my own negative thoughts were causing it. I thought there had to be someone out there who could fix me. A magic pill, maybe? There had to be something. I found a few amazing people, who are still in my life, that helped me understand anxiety and negative thoughts. It did not happen overnight. It took me two solid years of practicing the tools that have helped me. Not everyone may take that long to get better, but I was really good at the negative talk!

THINGS THAT HELPED ME

Over the years of my recovery, I tried anything that I thought could possibly help me. I started going for walks and taking yoga and meditation classes. I know that yoga can really help with anxiety, but with me having a full-time job and two small kids at home, it was not easy for me to get to yoga class enough to see a huge difference. I did, however, start meditating. I would set my timer on my phone and meditate for at least five to ten minutes a day. Meditating is hard in the beginning, I had major monkey brain! I cannot focus on anything very long, but guided meditations really helped that problem. I still do the guided meditations or try to sit quietly for a few minutes here and there throughout the day.

The biggest thing that helped was positive affirmations. I had them hanging on my bathroom mirror, on the refrigerator, and popping up every hour on my phone. They were very simple sayings such as, "We are safe, we are okay." On my bathroom mirror, I had them where I saw them first thing in the morning. I would read them a few times to myself. They would read, "You are amazing, you are beautiful." This is an amazing way to start your day. Beginning the day in a positive, loving way is always the right way.

I started journaling. I journal everyday, sometimes twice a day. I always liked writing in a journal, but I never realized how powerful it is. I start off every entry of my journal with writing what I am grateful for. I will be honest, some days it might be hard to find something to be grateful for, especially during the beginning of your recovery. On those hard days, I would simply write, "I am grateful for my breath," or, "I am so happy and grateful for the beautiful sky." Every single thing around us is something to be grateful for! After I write what I am grateful for, I write out my list of things I want to accomplish and things I have accomplished in my life. I just write a few things. It does not have to take very long. I will also write out the way I want things to go. For instance, I recently went on a trip with my family. I wrote out how the trip was going to go. I wrote that we would have amazing flights, plenty of laughs and fun, and memories made. That is exactly what happened! I have learned that putting out to the Universe what you want is exactly what you get!

Finally, I started to pray. Pray to who or what you believe in. I believe in God, I trust Him, and I asked Him for help. "Please God, help me. I cannot live this way, and I know you did not bring me to this Earth and give me these beautiful children, just for me to not enjoy them."

MY MISSION

It has been about a full year now of feeling so much better. During my time of feeling anxious and depressed, I would think to myself, "Nobody should ever feel like this. I am going to help them." I have, through the years, helped many clients of mine, not only from my own experience but from my mom's experience. I was with her during some of her panic attacks many years ago. Even though I had not actually experienced it in my body, I was witness to her having them and knew how to help my clients or friends dealing with panic. Ironic, right? That I was in total denial that panic was happening to me!

I am dedicating my life to help others suffering, in any way I can. I love helping people feel more confident and more beautiful from the inside out. I am drawn to helping women figure out what they really want to do with their lives and how to achieve it. Confidence is the number one key ingredient in all of this. My job every day at the salon is to make women feel more beautiful and teach them to do their own hair and makeup so that they can achieve the look they want—and slay the day! I am also starting a coaching business where I teach clients all of the tools they need to be more confident, overcome anxiety, and feel beautiful from the inside out.

I am so grateful for the anxiety and panic that I had. It has taught me so much. It has shown me who I want to be and how to be it. I am also so grateful for the tools I now have to help me when anxiety and panic try to sneak in. Because believe me, they try to a lot. Anxiety knows not to mess with now!

I wish each and everyone one of you peace, love, and joy in your life every day. May peace prevail.

Love you,
Mandy Scanlon

ABOUT MANDY SCANLON

Mandy Scanlon is a #1 Best Selling Author, Certified Ignitor Coach, Speaker, Stylist, and owns an online boutique. Mandy has a passion for helping men and women feel more beautiful and healing themselves from the inside out. Mandy often does makeovers on women who have done amazing things in her community and are not seeing that they are in need of self care. Mandy coaches them while they are receiving a makeup application, hairstyle, and advice on which pieces of clothing look the best on their body type.

Mandy is in the process of beginning an etiquette and style school for children. Mandy has two children, ages ten and six, and knows how important is for children to have confidence and self-love and wants to teach them the tools to always be confident in any situation.

Mandy invites you to contact her at mandyscanlon.com
Facebook: Mandy Midili Scanlon
Facebook group: Confidence + Clothing
Instagram: @Mandy_Scanlon

LIVING IN LIGHT

Alicia Thorp

Being on the go, having the freedom to do what I pleased, filling my calendar up, having a busy daily schedule with friends and fun activities was how I lived my life. I was attracted to people who also lived and loved that lifestyle. As I settled down into a relationship, where I was used to having freedom and being active, I found myself with a different perception of my life. I realized I was living, trying to be everything for everyone, forgetting to even begin to sit and truly know what it was like to live for me.

In my mid-twenties, when I found out I was going to be a mother for the first time, my life changed, and my mindset shifted. I was in a relationship that was carefree and active, but life told me to slow down for my body that was creating a nurturing space for this baby inside of me. As I began to slow down and really listen to what my body needed, I was able to take a step back and honestly assess what was most important. I realized that what I needed to focus on most was caring for myself and my baby, instead of always being everywhere for everyone else. My priorities shifted and I was now starting to focus inward instead of looking for activities that kept me busy. This new mindset created some disconnects; it changed me, and it changed my relationship. As I adapted to these shifts, I began to feel that tension was building in my relationship. I was at my happiest knowing I was creating a magical life inside me, even though simultaneously, my relationship and my marriage stopped progressing in the same way it once was.

A darkness started to reveal itself in my marriage during this time. Prior to me slowing down, this darkness was not something that I encountered. I was consumed by this new and drastic change; it altered my life forever. The communication started to break down in my marriage and it transformed into aggressive conversations. Those conversations warped into arguments, which became loud and scary. The arguments went from verbal aggression and put-downs to slamming doors, throwing objects, and even physical aggression. This was no longer a carefree relationship and I began feeling lost. I was living with a new perception of life and I noticed that this darkness was taking me to my lowest point. Internally, I was in turmoil. I fought negative self-talk and started to believe that crying, every single day, was going to be my life. If I didn't stick through the hard times, I was selfish for not trying harder. I was going through the motions of life, people-pleasing, just to make it through another day. There was so much friction and tension building up that I wasn't sure I was strong enough to make the changes that I knew deep down in my gut were needed. I was unraveling.

I began to see my relationship with eyes wide open for the first time and I knew this could not continue. It would not be easy or quick, but I needed to release myself from the darkness. I was ready to figure out a way to redefine myself. It was time to find my light through this journey that brought in an unexpected darkness. It was time to love myself and trust my intuition so I could shine the brightest. This is my journey of spiritual growth and living in light.

As I stepped out into life following my new mindset, I felt like I was starting over. I was ready to move forward intentionally for me and my baby, and I knew the time had come for me to make a conscious change to fully embrace my life. It was up to me to find peace from my darkness and move forward in a positive light. I realized that I was always keeping myself so busy, so I didn't have to go inward and truly figure out how to live as my true self. I was so used to being on the go and being active that I was making a point not to be still. That familiar active lifestyle would no longer serve me, I was not grounded in who I was—it was time to get grounded. I began to explore living in the moment, being present and living with awareness. Taking life at a slower pace and nurturing myself in the present moment was not selfish or wrong, but necessary. I began to find it acceptable to slow down and to pursue activities for myself without fear of being judged by others. I realized it was time to say 'yes' to me, and I could say 'no' to others.

I had to find a healthy balance and rebuild myself. I paid closer attention to my decisions, especially since becoming a new mom. The turning point for me was saying no to an event, without guilt. I was invited, as I had been previously, but I knew from attending in years past that I would be helping set up and break down. I knew that I would be out late, and I would be running around making sure everyone was happy. I had, in that moment, felt something new: it was the need to be grounded and, in that present moment, I finally realized what being grounded was all about. I was able to see that opportunity of no. I felt the shift in my body and instead of jumping on this invite to fill my day, I said no. No! Such a small word with so much power. It was terrifying yet liberating to hear myself put myself first. I accepted the need to be grounded in my decisions. It was freeing. I lost some friends throughout this transition, but I also gained more clarity and ultimately a life of love and light. I slowly started to love myself fearlessly and saw that people-pleasing did not feel good to me. I was happiest living in the moments that mattered most, the moments of my life. I was ready for growth that felt good and was ready to live in alignment with my truth.

As I noticed my thoughts and my feelings more, I embraced everything that came to me, even if I didn't fully understand it in that moment. I wasn't used to feeling emotions behind my actions, but as I embraced my new lifestyle, I recognized that the emotions I felt were my internal guidance and intuition. I was being guided on this new path in my life and I was listening. I began to learn that my intuition was the strongest indicator of living in alignment as my true self. When I felt good, I knew that my actions were guiding me into what was best for me. When I felt uncomfortable, I was able to embrace that feeling and acknowledge that what I was doing was not in alignment for me. It took some time, but I accepted that it was okay to change my mind. I started to accept myself and I began to take back control of my life. It was with this that I fully accepted I had a dark past, but that did not have to define how bright I could make my future.

There was peace in my life and new doors opened for me. I began taking yoga classes since I heard it was good for strength. After a few classes, I noticed a serenity throughout my whole body. This amazing new feeling gave me the confidence to do more than to just go to a yoga class. I had to share this amazing practice, I had to teach others. I allowed my internal guidance to lead the way and I enrolled in yoga teacher training. Yoga felt good to my body and mind. My yoga practice allowed me to connect more deeply to my thoughts. I was able to notice disconnects that were created in my mind from my past relationship. For the first time in a long time, I felt free to be me. I was feeling more empowered in my life than ever before. I released past dark thoughts and feelings so I could embrace and welcome in my light. I was growing in confidence and I was finally ready to live life, on my terms.

Living in light, in my personal power, gave me that jolt of awareness I needed to see all the miracles and magic that surrounded me. I was gaining more mental and physical strength daily. I was owning my life, both my past and the present, for the first time. I was showing up as the brightest version of myself for those who I loved. I made major shifts in my mindset and it allowed me to see that the way I was living in the past was to serve others without connecting with myself. That was not how I was meant to live. I accepted that my life did not have to be understood by everyone. Finding this deeper, more true connection with myself led me to live more in the present moments without the fear and judgment that once surrounded me. I embraced my daily awareness with appreciation, love, and gratitude. When I allowed gratitude to enter my life, I released expectations and I was presented with opportunities effortlessly.

Gratitude became a critical part of my life as it guided me to give thanks in all areas. I used gratitude daily to transform the negativity I had experienced into a strength and a point of growth. Gratitude and thanks kept me grounded with what was important. When I woke up every morning, before I even stepped out of bed, I would state five things I was grateful for. My gratitude practice grew from there and is still something I practice daily. Being thankful gives me the ability to grow, build strength, be empowered, and to see my experiences in life as a lesson.

I was consciously aware of my thoughts and actions as I continued to make a daily effort to journey through my life in awareness and gratitude. I embraced the fact that I could be in control of my life. I was able to let go of negative connections and old patterns that the past darkness had on me. My life experiences evolved my world into something more amazing and beautiful than I could have ever imagined. I embraced my life, my child, my love of yoga, my feelings, my intuition and daily gratitude with my whole heart. Showing up for my life in my true power led me to have peaceful awareness of my past darkness, acknowledgment of my present light, and the ability of living a life where I can constantly expand my future with pure gratitude.

Today I am loved and fully supported. I make conscious decisions daily that enhance my life. I show up for every moment. I live a life that is in alignment for me and in the highest and greatest good for my family. My husband, who I dedicate my spiritual growth to, constantly brightens my life and fills my soul with love. I have enhanced my life by being present, living in alignment, and showing gratitude every single day. I invite you to embrace your life, sit with your thoughts, be here now, inhale, exhale, share gratitude, and live in your light.

ABOUT ALICIA THORP

About Alicia Thorp

Alicia Thorp is a certified mindfulness practitioner, Reiki practitioner and yoga instructor. Combining her certifications and life experiences, she is pursuing her passion as a mindset mentor. Alicia's mentoring will leave you feeling empowered and ready to live life as the brightest version of yourself. Being a domestic violence survivor empowered Alicia to become a wellness advocate. Alicia is providing support to others using mindful awareness by implementing specific strategies, such as the importance of living in the present moment. Alicia is a spiritual entrepreneur with a nurturing and heart-centered soul and is passionate about helping others retrain their mindset.

Alicia is growing her business as an author, speaker, and mindset mentor while working full-time with special needs adults. She has been featured in Facebook interviews and podcasts about mindset and mindfulness since becoming certified in 2016. She is currently residing in Southern New Jersey with her husband, children, and cats. She enjoys coffee, fresh flowers, and being in nature.

You can connect with Alicia on Facebook at Facebook.com/AliciaThorp or online at AliciaThorp.com

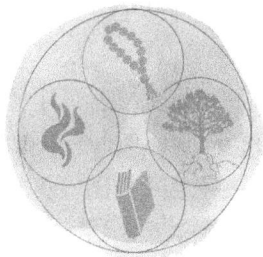

FOLLOW YOUR HEART

Gina Walton

No matter how you outwardly compare us, Edwin and I are different. We are not the same age, gender, ethnicity, or socio-economic status. At the time we met, I was a fifty-two-year-old, white, middle class married woman living in the suburbs, and he was a young twenty-year-old Puerto Rican man, homeless and unemployed. Yet, fate brought us together seven years ago and what has unfolded since then has been a soul to soul connection and a journey together that I couldn't have imagined. I have seen how the ripple effect of love has spread out as our friendship has grown and as others have been touched by our story.

I was about two years into my spiritual journey when I met Edwin. As part of my healing and recovery from a bout with post-traumatic stress disorder, I was led by a dear friend to a book called *Ask and it is Given* by Esther and Jerry Hicks. This book had a profound effect on me. As I read it, it resonated so deeply, and it satisfied my long-held desire for a real spiritual connection to a Higher Power. It became the springboard from which I dove into the spiritual and metaphysical realms. Over the years that have followed, I have devoured many books on spirituality, attended a variety of classes, joined a spiritual center and have become very deliberate about integrating all that I have been learning into my life and into my relationships.

During this period, I also discovered and pursued my passion for numerology, which is the occult study of the significance of numbers. I have since been able to help many people over the years by using the universal language of numbers to reveal to them their life's blueprint. My readings help to empower people to live in harmony with their soul's purpose and to better understand their strengths and challenges. In addition, they become aware of the cyclical influence of numbers on their lives which enables them to live in a better flow with those energetic influences. It has been very rewarding for me to help to shed light in this way for others.

The past ten years have really felt like a spiritual boot camp in which I have been amassing the tools and building the spiritual muscle to enable me to cultivate my faith and to stay resilient in the face of whatever comes along. In 2012, a Universal Year of "change", Edwin came along.

He is the same age as my own son but, again, that's where the similarity ended. At twenty years of age, he was a high school drop-out and already an unmarried father to three young children! "How was this possible?" I wondered. My curiosity about his situation led me to ask more, and while he temporarily worked at my home, I got to know more about him, his children, and their mom, Lizzette. I cannot say that our outer differences or the circumstances around the children were what solely drove my curiosity because I know now that there were larger forces at play and that we were destined to meet and to learn from each other.

Extending kindness and compassion to others is one important way that we demonstrate our belief in unity consciousness. However, we are ineffective in our ability to help another if we focus solely on their outer circumstances and deem them to be incapable of "righting their own ship". In this state, we are viewing them from a place of our own disconnection where we can be of little real service. I learned this lesson as I began to "help" Edwin. I wanted things for him that he didn't even dare to want for himself. I had ideas about how to help him, his children, and their mother, sometimes taking responsibility for things that were not my responsibility and then expecting gratitude in return. Little did I know that the Universe had its own plan for Edwin's growth, a plan that would naturally result in my own evolution as well.

What happened was a fatal car crash early on Easter morning in 2014. Edwin had been drinking and got behind the wheel of a car with his girlfriend, Tiffany, after an altercation with another man at a bar. He caused an accident in which he and Tiffany were both thrown from the car and Tiffany died at the scene. Edwin also nearly died but was revived in the ambulance. After recovering from his injuries, he was taken into custody and was eventually sentenced to serve eight and a half years in prison for vehicular homicide. My heart went out to him because so many things that he loved were lost as a result of his reckless behavior: his girlfriend, his job, his home, time with his family and children, and his freedom.

The significance of the accident occurring on Easter morning, however, was not lost on me. I knew that Edwin's revival in that ambulance could be viewed as an opportunity for his own spiritual rebirth. After he had been in prison for several months, I received a letter from him. On the back of the letter was a beautiful drawing of two hands holding a heart. It said, "I am so sorry."

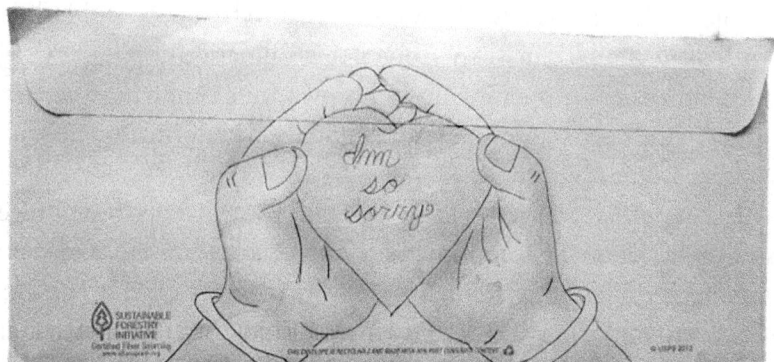

In that letter, he admitted that he had a problem with alcohol that went back to his early teen years. He was attending weekly AA meetings in prison that were helping him. He vowed to never be who he used to be, to better his life, and to be the best person possible for his family. He vowed to become a speaker and to share this story with others as a warning about the dangers of drinking and driving. He thanked me for all I had done for him and his children and their mom. Then, he asked me to forgive him and asked me if I would be willing to write back to him. His letter touched me deeply and I wrote back to him to say that, yes, he had my forgiveness. I encouraged him to work toward self-forgiveness for all that had happened and all that he had lost. This is where our journey together began again.

Over the years that have followed, our friendship has deepened, and we have each grown as a result. Edwin's letters to me continued to come with beautiful hand-drawn art on the outside of the envelopes and news of how he was changing on the inside. In return, I wrote to him and sent him many books, encouraging him to expand his self-awareness and his thinking. It was during his weekly AA meetings where he first realized the power of telling his story. My heart overflowed with joy from the insights and revelations that he wrote about. He told me how the chaplain there had become a friend and a mentor. This man had hidden talents in the sense that he could easily tap into the voice of Spirit and the message for Edwin was that he was destined to be a powerful influence on others as he told his story. To get this validation was so rewarding for Edwin as he was opening up to his own inner knowing, which was coming in the form of dreams, visions, and inside information pertaining to others around him there.

After months of corresponding by mail, I worked up the courage to visit Edwin. Knowing someone in prison was a first for me, and visiting someone in prison was definitely out of my comfort zone! It was a relief to see firsthand, though, that Edwin was doing fine. I could tell after a few visits that he had the respect of the corrections officers and that was validation for me that he had been showing them respect as well. Within the confines of prison, this young man was finding his way and so appreciative of the interest I showed in him and the time that I spent helping him. What he didn't realize was that he was helping me as well. Our relationship was helping my need to express all of the things that I had been learning about myself and the spiritual path that I was on. It was a great opportunity for me to "walk the walk".

Edwin's art, which he made with very limited resources, became a real inspiration to me. I needed to complete a creative project for a class that I was taking but I was not at all confident in my creative ability. I knew, however, from learning about my own numerology that self-expression and creativity (which were sadly lacking in my life) would feed my soul. Spirit whispered to me, "Start by using Edwin's drawings to create something." What came from that was a beautiful collage that I made using torn copies of Edwin's drawings and a torn-up copy of the newspaper article about his accident. It was an unplanned image of a person rising from the flames (created from his drawings) amidst the ashes (created from the article about the accident). It was divinely inspired and to create it so effortlessly felt like pure magic!

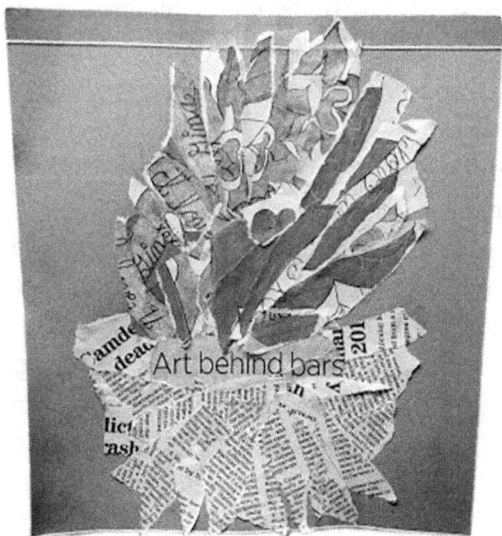

From that project, I began to use watercolors to paint. I used scans of my work to create notecards and it felt amazing to create something useful from my own paintings. I used my cards when I wrote to Edwin and he encouraged me to keep painting. I know now that we are all capable of being artistic and I have cultivated an acceptance and appreciation of the art that I create, allowing it to come forth as it wishes. In addition, Edwin embraced my passion for numerology and enjoyed it when I shared my insights about what the numbers in his life's blueprint revealed about him. I will be forever grateful to him for inspiring my own creativity and for encouraging me to pursue my passion for numerology.

With over half of his sentence completed and no discipline issues, Edwin was recently able to transfer to the Full Minimum-Security Unit of the facility where he has more freedom. Upon his intake interview, he met with the head of the unit and got the opportunity to tell her his story. She realized that he was not like other inmates in that he took full responsibility for the actions that led to his current circumstances. He was passionate and emotional as he told her of his plan to share his story to help others by participating in the prison's Project P.R.I.D.E program (Promoting Responsibility in Drug Education). In this program, inmates travel to schools to share their stories of how drug use has impacted their lives.

The head of the unit was actually moved to tears as he told her that his time in prison has truly been a blessing as it stopped him from continuing down the wrong path. To his delight, she told him that she recognizes in him the gift to "move" others that all great motivational speakers possess. She told him that she "hoped to see him out there" someday! He was able to witness, again, the impact of speaking from his heart. Listening to him recount this experience with amazement as we visited left me feeling in awe of how wonderfully Spirit can orchestrate these watershed moments for us. My heart swelled with pride for him.

I left after our visit that day knowing that this young man is on the road to great things. He is undergoing his own training there in prison and I am confident that Spirit will not have him there one day longer than is necessary. He has moments, of course, when he gets disheartened, loses faith in the process and loses patience with the system. He knows, though, that he has come too far in his thinking and made too much progress on his path towards change to do anything but soldier on. He has been able to cultivate a sense of inner freedom in a place where there is little outward freedom. He tells the story of his accident with real courage and with a deep desire to inspire others to learn from his mistakes. It is also a way in which he honors the memory of his girlfriend, Tiffany, and atones for her death.

The first few months of participating in the Project P.R.I.D.E program have been life-changing for Edwin. Through his courage and his vulnerability in sharing his story, he has made an emotional connection with so many in the audience as he goes out to various schools to speak. The impact of his story can really be felt during the question and answer period after he speaks. He thoroughly enjoys being in the spotlight on stage and he is articulate in his delivery. He has spoken at local middle and high schools, vocational-technical schools, and universities, including Princeton University!

He is now poised to embody his full potential as he gets ready to take his G.E.D exam and I know that many good things will continue to follow. My heart is full of love and gratitude for this young man. I am able to take his three children (ages ten, nine, and seven) on the long trip to visit him every few months as I maintain a good relationship with their mother and can help her in this way. His children are so happy to see their dad as he is to see them. Edwin is so appreciative of the time that I take to do this and it's always wonderful for me to witness their reunions and to play a part in that joy.

It has been a real honor and privilege to be on this journey with Edwin and I am so grateful for the way in which Spirit orchestrated our "chance" meeting and gave me the courage to follow my heart. I have learned so much from this young man and he inspires me every day with his courage, his honesty, his willingness to grow and change, and his desire to be a beacon of light for others as I have been for him. He has learned the importance of forgiveness, self-love, and self-respect and has shown through the embodiment of these practices that one can survive and even thrive under the most difficult circumstances. I believe that this experience is leading Edwin toward his life's purpose which is to use his voice to uplift and inspire others who may find themselves in what they consider to be hopeless circumstances.

In sharing our story, I encourage you to not be afraid to follow your heart or to leave your comfort zone when it comes to helping others. We are all a part of the same human family and are not separate from each other on a soul level. What heals and uplifts one person helps to heal and uplift us all. It is my desire to be of service to the Divine in this way, one person at a time, whether it be with a numerology reading, a letter, or a visit in prison. I may not always see the ripple effects that go outward from my actions, but I know that they are there, and I have faith that I am helping to illuminate the world as a result. For that, I am grateful and truly fulfilled in my own life's purpose.

ABOUT GINA WALTON

Gina Walton lives in New Jersey with her husband and soulmate, David, of thirty-four years. She is a nurturer at heart, with a special love for children and a desire to help educate and empower them. She loves being on the leading-edge of thought, especially with respect to spiritual ideas. Her deeper interest lies in using her voice to help give voice to those who may be without a voice. She is passionate about the field of numerology and has been using it as a tool with others to help shed light on their propensities, capabilities, talents, and challenges.

Look for her next book, *Baby Talk: The Top 10 Things Your Newborn Wants You to Know*, which will be published soon on Amazon.com. It is a loving, soul-based parenting guide that provides spiritual insights on how to best help children thrive as they grow. It gives babies a voice in those early years and reminds parents that our children are each born with a unique blueprint, a strong connection to the spiritual realm, and the ability to help teach us to learn and grow.

To connect with Gina or to inquire about a numerology reading, you can reach her at IDoYourNumbers@gmail.com.

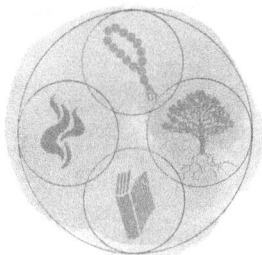

UP LIKE ROSES

Katie Wood

I had a boss once who told me I could fall into a pile of shit and come out smelling like roses. I didn't know if I should take that as a compliment or an insult, because it sounded like a good thing, but he was also kind of an asshole. I guess you could say this "up like roses" analogy was true in my life, especially during my earlier years. Despite having a sister with special needs who was in and out of the hospital for long periods of time, I had a fairly normal childhood. There were family vacations, campouts in the backyard, holiday gatherings, and concerts performed for stuffed animals.

The roses followed me to college, where I studied International & Community Development. I didn't really know much about the major, but it allowed me the most opportunities to travel and I loved the sound of that. I took trips to Australia, El Salvador, Los Angeles, St. Louis, Grand Rapids, and South Africa for conferences, mission trips, and internships. It was also through this major that I met my husband and we shared reams of living overseas and working with vulnerable populations. Our college motto was "Be a World Changer," which evoked an underlying sense of pressure to have big dreams and accomplish greatness immediately after graduation.

I soon learned, however, that reality was not a kindred spirit to those

221

expectations. As a young newlywed couple, we were filled with fire and ambition that was only matched by the amount of student loan debt we carried. Our application to join the Peace Corps was quickly denied because we owned the equivalent of a house, a boat, and a nice car in student loan debt. I was faced with the hard truth that my dreams and reality were at odds and I couldn't do both the way I had pictured. I made the slow choice to sacrifice my dreams in order to live in the real world—but it didn't really feel like a choice at all. My life became a cycle of pulling excuses like covers over my head and pushing the snooze button on my life for what seemed like the hundredth time before rolling over into a new day. Sometimes the dreams and "world changer" expectations would creep up only for me to push them back down so I could get through the day, meet the deadline, go home to fix dinner, and do it all over again.

What might be considered the ideal "white picket fence" life for some felt like surrender mixed with a little bit of failure to me. We moved back to my hometown of Madison, Indiana and I got a job. It was a daily battle after college to settle down without feeling like I had settled. Instead of living overseas in a hut feeding orphans, I was living in a small town working part-time at the Boys & Girls Club—I had to intentionally find the roses in order to stop and smell them.

While I wasn't living every alternative version of my life the way I had envisioned, it wasn't long before I found purpose in Madison. It came in the form of the Ulster Project—a month long summer exchange right in my hometown! The Project's mission is to help young potential leaders from the US and Northern Ireland become peacemakers by providing a safe environment to learn and practice the skills needed to unite people when differences divide them. In Madison, the Project pairs twelve local fifteen-year-olds with counterparts from Enniskillen, Northern Ireland. The group of twenty-four spends the month of July attending multi-denominational religious services, performing serving projects, participating in peace education called Time of Discovery, and having an all-around life changing experience.

In 2009, I started out as a counselor, leading the group on their daily activities. The following year, my husband and I took over the local organization as volunteer co-presidents and were soon asked to join the international steering committee. Together, we launched a leadership development curriculum that was implemented by other Projects across the country. We also traveled to Ireland to present at the international conference. Ulster was our baby. It became everything we felt like we were missing before—our church, our community, our family, and a place to throw our passion and watch the fruits of our labor blossom year after year. It was an all-consuming storm, but we were facing it together. The problem was that it was all volunteer and we had to keep up with our careers as well.

We fell into a routine with all of this. We relied on each other and on the team of people we had gathered around us. During the Project each July, it wasn't uncommon for us to wake up early, put in a full day at work, go straight to an Ulster event where we would lead an activity or manage a crisis, and then come home to crash after 11:00 pm. In fact, almost every day of the month looked like this. Ironically, the energy we got every July fueled us for the rest of the year. I had found my roses.

It was all the perfect set up—until it wasn't. I found out I was pregnant the day of the first meeting that kicked off the 2014 Ulster season. I remember shaking as I stood at the front of the room, realizing that everything I knew was about to change. I'll skip the details of my pregnancy and the birth of our son. What I want to talk about here is how lost I felt in the overwhelm of becoming a new mother. There were times when I didn't think I could do it. It all seemed like too much—too much pressure, too much responsibility, too much love, too many big feelings. I was a strong and successful woman, dammit. How was I being defeated by a tiny human?

The struggle was real and so were my defense mechanisms. I found that it was easier for me to numb my emotions, so I didn't have to face the pain of not being able to "handle it" all. Instead of letting go of the things that were no longer serving me, I clung tightly to anything that resembled my old life—back when I had it all together. I became good at wearing masks and dulling the pain. In a very clumsy attempt to juggle everything, I slowly started to resent the things I used to love. All of my numbing of the pain and the struggle had also stolen my joy. It was a downward spiral; I was swirling in uncertainty without a plan. Looking back, this was probably a form of postpartum depression, but it was definitely unrecognized at the time.

I went back to work after a short maternity leave and threw myself into growing programs on a regional level. I was trying to prove that I was still strong and capable—that my value hadn't diminished even though I struggled to see it in myself. I felt like I was failing in every area of my life. I found solace in the words of my boss at the time. He later became a mentor and dear friend with a reflective wisdom that always made me feel like I had known the answers all along. His encouragement and guidance allowed me to see possibilities that existed in my future that were otherwise lost in the swirl. He was my go-to person—the one I would text when I had a question about which light bulbs to buy or how to properly soak chickpeas when making hummus. He was also there for the big stuff like applying for jobs, buying my first home, and deciding to go back to school. I can still hear his voice telling me, "In two years the same amount of time will have passed and you'll either have your degree or you won't."

Halfway through my first year of grad school, I got a call that shook me to my core. My friend and mentor had committed suicide. I remember exactly where I was, what I was wearing, what meal I had just eaten. The days and weeks that followed were all a blur, but those details are preserved in my mind. What came next was an overwhelming darkness. There was no swirl, definitely no roses—I couldn't even see the pile of shit I was paralyzed in. When he died, it felt like all of my answers died with him. The sense of overwhelm had been replaced by a giant void in front of me that I just couldn't see around.

A few months later, my husband and I found out we were expecting our second child. What should have been a time of pure joy and excitement was clouded by grief and anxiety over the possibility of losing someone else I loved. My mentor started visiting me in my dreams and answering questions I didn't even know I had. I moved through the stages of grief, but I couldn't seem to make it to the final stage of acceptance. When my daughter was born, the shit hit the fan. All of my old ways of hiding and numbing my feelings came flooding back. The postpartum depression was definitely real this time and once again, I was in denial.

When she was born, I stepped down from almost every role that had previously defined me. I left the workforce completely, was no longer involved with the Ulster Project, and cut off nearly every connection I had with friends outside of my parents and my husband. It took everything I had in me to get out of bed and take care of my basic needs while keeping my new baby alive. Throw a toddler with sleep regression and a husband who was launching a new career into the mix and you can almost hear my mental collapse.

I remember waking up one day thinking, "How did I get here? Is this the life I want to be living?" The hard answer was an emphatic no, and with that an overwhelming flood of guilt. My American-dream life left me feeling unfulfilled, unhappy, and unable to change it. A friend visited around this time and had a tough conversation with me that changed everything. It was like she held up a mirror, forcing me to look inward to find a true awareness about who I was and how I got there. Her words called me out of my place of hiding and challenged me to get my emotional shit together so I could pour into my relationships from the overflow. The next few months were a blur, but in a different way than the void or the swirl of overwhelm I had known before. This sparked my journey of rediscovering who I am and rebuilding my life around the dreams that have always been inside of me.

It started with asking the tough questions. So, you're feeling unfulfilled.

Why? You think there has to be something more. Why? You're judging yourself for leaving the workforce to be a stay-at-home-mom. Why? The biggest question was, "What is the void that is holding you back from contentment?" The answer came in a moment of clarity—growth. I had stopped reaching for growth because I thought I had already achieved the things on my list (husband, home, family, career, meaningful work, etc.) which meant I could just stop trying. I had reached my goals without really celebrating them or replacing them with new ones. Perhaps my former roses had matured, and it was time to re-plant.

Once I had this revelation, it was a snowball of personal growth. I got back to the core of who I am. Without defining myself as a mother, wife, daughter, sister, friend, teacher, etc. I dug down to the root of what I want to be about—my core values. Once those were clearly defined, I could start saying no to things that were outside of those areas. Up until this point in my life, the word "no" was rarely in my vocabulary. I was giving away important pieces of myself without gaining anything of value in return. This act of strengthening the power of my "yes" has been a game changer! Now I can show up well to the things I am committed to and act as the best version of myself.

After I realized I didn't like the way my life looked, I broke it down into the seemingly insignificant habits that made up my day. I made a list of everything I didn't like and wrote down every reason I could think of to explain why I did it. For example, I watched too much TV during the day. Why? Because I missed adult voices. Because I wanted to escape to a different reality. Because I was bored. So, what could I do instead? To fill the same needs, I started listening to podcasts. I chose ones with positive messages about growth and development, which shifted the focus of my brain. I replaced social media scrolling with reaching out to actual friends to fill the loneliness void. I replaced resting on the couch with walks outside to move my body and breathe in some fresh air. I started every morning with a gratitude journal and some positive affirmations. These tiny adjustments began to shift my entire reality. Nothing had changed about my circumstances. The only thing that was different was me and how I chose to show up. I went from dreading the long days at home alone with a baby to looking forward to the opportunity to learn new things and put new habits in place.

It has been about a year since the mirror was held up to me. I am a different person than the shell of a woman who was reflected back then. I barely recognize her. I am now confident, inspired, and full of dreams and plans for the future. I am coming up like roses in a way I never thought possible. I am leaning into my "next" of endless possibilities instead of swirling in the overwhelm of uncertainty. I have surrounded myself with people who remind me to stay focused and inspired. I finished my master's program in May, and I find myself at another crossroad. This time, however, the only thing I have to prove is that I am open and ready to receive. I am no longer paranoid by lack—either in myself or my career opportunities. I have a grounded trust that things are working out for the highest and best of all involved, even if it seems out of my control.

After all these years, I decided to look up the "up like roses" phrase. The wise Google machine gave the following definition: "To result in success or an exceptionally good outcome, especially in the face of doubts or difficulties." I cannot think of a better way to describe this journey I've been on throughout my life. This new awareness of coming up like roses has been a reminder that whatever my "next" is, I will face it with a steady confidence that the universe always has my back.

ABOUT KATIE WOOD

Adventurous and passionate, Katie is the mother of two and teaches business classes for IU East and Ivy Tech. She was instrumental in developing the student success class at Ivy Tech and loves teaching others to reach their full potential. She just accepted a new position at Hanover College, and looks forward to helping students there succeed in their academic endeavors and on their quest for a more fulfilling life.

She is passionate about relationships and enjoys helping others examine themselves and make course corrections in their lives. Through her blogs and other social media posts, in the classroom, and in her relationships, Katie exudes a passion for life that others recognize and aspire to attain. When she's not working or volunteering, you can find her strolling the neighborhood with her family, chasing sunsets, binge-watching *House Hunters International*, or exploring new cities. This chapter was written during and inspired by one of the busiest years of her life—new baby, finishing her MBA, hosting an exchange student, and working hard on personal development. Katie has her parents to thank for teaching her the value of community, diversity, inclusion, grace, and growth. It is her mission to always chase the sunny side of life and build others up along the way.

You can find her on Instagram @kwood31 or online at www.twowoodsinc.com.

AN UNEXPECTED OPPORTUNITY

Sondra Wyckoff

Check! Is there a better feeling than checking something off of your to-do list? I am driven by developing a plan and completing a task in all aspects of life. Managing my day, making plans with friends, and coordinating my week with my husband, I find that I can accomplish the most when I have a clear set plan that I can execute.

Throughout my life I was often called a "go-getter". I'm naturally curious and eager to learn new things and always trust my gut instincts in any situation. From a young age I took on leadership positions by being captain of my youth cheerleading team at age seven, serving as class secretary at age thirteen, and becoming president of the marketing club in college. Every decision I made was researched and well thought out, and I had a hand in determining the outcome.

I can think of a handful of exceptions to this in my life. One exception was when my husband proposed to me. We had been having serious discussions about our future and landed on a timeline of three years before we would be getting engaged and ready to start our future. Three days later he proposed.

Once we settled into marriage, we kicked off another planning session, this time about when we wanted to start a family. Both career-driven and independent, we thought that we would take our time, but at the

229

same time we would leave it up to fate. If we ended up being pregnant earlier than expected then we would embrace it, knowing that we plan, and God laughs. So, with that thought in mind, I stopped taking birth control.

My gut instinct and decision-making skills that are second nature started to kick in to high gear when shortly after I stopped taking birth control, I started to notice a rapid weight gain and significant change in my skin. I investigated by booking an appointment with a general care practitioner who recommended that I track my food and activity intake and to come back in a month. This was not something I was unfamiliar with, and I made a promise to myself that I would track absolutely everything that I was eating and stick to thirty minutes of activity a day.

When I went to my follow up appointment with no change in my weight, I was discouraged when I was scolded by the doctor that I wasn't putting in enough effort and must have been doing something wrong. This was the first of a series of appointments where I heard, "Maybe you should try a meal replacement shake," "Are you feeling stressed about anything?" "Are you in a happy marriage?" All in response to questions about my menstrual cycle, rapid weight gain, and all overlooking the fact that I had not been taking birth control for four years and was not getting pregnant.

All the while, I began to listen to my gut and do my own research. I was learning about endocrine disruptors in everyday household items, hormonal changes, and how this can all impact fertility. It was through this research and thorough intuition that I knew there would be a medical professional out there who could answer my questions. I just had to find them.

After one particularly frustrating appointment, I reached out to a close friend who shared the same OBGYN as me. She expressed similar frustrations about the office and their bedside manner and attentiveness. She told me about this amazing doctor she had been hearing about who was starting her own practice and wanted to focus on more personalized care for women. Sign. Me. Up. I signed up for their newsletter and stalked my inbox awaiting the news that this new practice was open.

I counted down the days for my appointment, consulted my husband, and we put together an extensive list of questions in preparation for the appointment. Days before the appointment we got a call from the doctor's office stating that they did not accept our insurance. I was devastated. I decided I would pay anything to have an opportunity to meet with this doctor.

When I walked into the office (ten minutes late, I will add. I might be a planner, but I am also an optimist. Optimistic people tend to be late), I was greeted by a cheerful woman who could tell I was frazzled by being late and told me it would be okay, and I wasn't late enough to lose my appointment. I was shocked. I had never walked into a place with such helpful and friendly staff.

When my name was called, I walked into a room with a table and chairs, not the exam table that I was used to facing. When the doctor walked in, I immediately knew I was in the right place. We clicked as if we were old friends and she listened to every single one of my questions and concerns. At the end of the conversation she said, "We need to get you some answers." It took everything I had not to burst into tears and hug her.

I then began my journey with a truly wonderful reproductive endocrinologist. With her practice, they ran numerous tests and blood work to determine what was stopping me from getting pregnant. All of the tests, by the way, were things I was learning about in my research. I finally found the professionals that could help me.

It was through this process that it was uncovered that I had fibroids on my thyroid, polyps and scar tissue in my uterus, as well as a completely closed right fallopian tube. I was then presented with my next steps in my journey to becoming a mother, which required surgery to remove my fallopian tube and starting the InVitro Fertilization (IVF) process.

When I first received the news, I was so relieved that we had found an answer to all of our questions. I didn't look at this as a burden or a hardship, I looked at it as an opportunity. That's not to say that my Type-A, checklist-making self wasn't completely thrown for a loop by this news. The optimist in me thought, finally, we were getting the opportunity to make our dreams of starting a family a reality. No more guessing, no more disappointment month after month. We had a plan—A PLAN!—and we knew what we needed to do.

When I told people the news, it was a mixed bag. Some shared stories of hope about people they knew who had success through IVF, but that did not comfort me. I was surprised that some of the people I was closest to responded with, "I'm so sorry you have to go through this," or, "I feel so guilty that I was able to have a child without any issues." I'm here to tell you that there is nothing to feel sorry or guilty about! Every woman is unique, and fertility is no exception. I feel so grateful to know that I will be able to have children through this astounding process of IVF.

One in eight couples have trouble getting pregnant or sustaining pregnancy (according to The National Infertility Association.) I didn't realize what this really meant until one Saturday morning when I had an ultrasound appointment leading up to my egg retrieval. The office opened at 7:00 AM, and I had planned to arrive as soon as the doors opened. When I arrived, much to my surprise, there were already several women outside the office doors, awaiting whatever news they came to receive that day. Once the doors opened, dozens more women came flooding through and so much emotion came over me. That day I realized how I have so many strong women walking this journey beside me, and I feel proud to be in their company.

I don't intend to depict that this journey has been easy. There have been many things that I have worked hard to overcome, like giving myself injections, becoming mentally tough even though deep down I wanted to give up. On several occasions, I have said out loud, "I can't wait for this to be over." Everyday tasks like remembering to take my medicine and give myself injections were just added to the pile, while trying to eat right, excel at work, be a good wife, be a good friend, be a good daughter, go to church, drink enough water—the list goes on. This is when you know that you need to take a timeout and meditate, do yoga, buy a new outfit, watch Netflix, get off social media; whatever your body is telling you that you need, you listen to it.

Waiting for results via phone call and email is very daunting and caused me a lot of anxiety. Especially after our first frozen embryo transfer did not result in a pregnancy. The beta results (a pregnancy test taken by blood test) showed a positive result, but my levels were lower than they expected. I had to go back for bloodwork every forty-eight hours, and it was a rollercoaster with levels doubling, then decreasing, and finally showing a negative result. We were heartbroken, and it took some time before we were ready to give it another go.

We still have six of our seven frozen embryos left and, as I write this, are preparing for our next frozen embryo transfer in the upcoming weeks. I have found an internal strength that I never experienced before and look to meditation, essential oils, and journaling to help me cope with all of the emotions that come with this season of my life.

It was my decision to take this journey by trusting my gut and working to get answers and find a solution. I have applied my instincts to so much more throughout my life whether in personal relationships, my career, and even my personal care by switching to chemical free products and natural and organic foods. I found opportunities to educate myself and make small changes in my life that make a big impact.

A mentor of mine says that in life there are no coincidences. I believe that with all of my heart. I wouldn't be here with all of you telling this story had it not been for my experience with IVF. I wanted to tell this story to let women who may be going through fertility issues to know they are not alone. I want them to know that they don't have to take the feedback they are given at face value. That they have a voice not only in their health and wellness, but in all aspects of life.

Through this journey I have found an even bigger opportunity to build a community and becoming a sounding board for women who are facing similar issues. There is a whole tribe of sisters behind you who know what you're going through, and I am one of them. It doesn't make you flawed, it doesn't make you less deserving to be a mother, it makes you you.

ABOUT SONDRA WYCKOFF

Sondra Wyckoff is a lifelong resident of Swedesboro, NJ. She loves making charcuterie boards and Sunday Brunch and spending time with her husband, Daniel, and two beagles, Rocco and Daisy. She graduated from Kutztown University of Pennsylvania with a Bachelor of Science, Business Administration majoring in Marketing. Sondra specializes in Direct to Consumer marketing and has worked for national brands in various industries including all-natural and organic foods, fashion apparel, and financial services.

Sondra has a passion for networking and connecting with like-minded people. She believes that women should feel empowered to educate themselves on health and wellness, as they are the decision-makers of their household. When you know better, you do better. Sondra aspires to build a community of women that support each other both personally and professionally. She has started a Facebook group, Fearless Femmes Facing Fertility, where women can share their struggles, questions, and enjoy each other's company while navigating their road to motherhood.

To connect with Sondra, visit www.sondrawyckoff.com
Instagram: @sondrawyckoff

Sondra is a patient of Reproductive Associates of Delaware (RAD). To learn more about them visit www.ivf-de.org.

I'M STILL STANDING

Eleni Yiambilis

There is a question I get asked on a regular basis: how are you always so happy, Eleni? Some ask with genuine curiosity while others ask in disbelief as if it's not possible. The most appropriate answer to that question is that life has given me a gratitude adjustment. Truthfully, I have learned through my personal experiences to feel blessed for each moment. There is something valuable to be taken from all of the circumstances life presents us. A lesson learned, inner strength, the ability to relate to others and help them through dark moments ... to illuminate. Like a phoenix from the ashes, the pain and struggles are the fuel to fly. Soaring with forgiveness and an open heart has led me to a life dedicated to service. This is where I have found my consistent happy place.

My childhood wasn't filled with gum drops, rainbows, and fun family memories. The house I grew up in was tainted with alcoholism and abuse in all forms. As a child I remember feeling it was my role to make everyone happy. My heart felt heavy with pressure and responsibility. The pressure to be perfect, to be the one to heal the family, to stop the yelling, to stop the broken dishes, to stop mom from crying, to protect my little brother from hearing the chaos. Thankfully, I did have a safe haven, St. George's restaurant. My family owned diners in Center City

237

Philadelphia and everyone there loved and treated me like family. Being part of this gave me a feeling of pride and a happier sense of purpose than I had at home. I spent every weekend and break from school there because it was the one place I felt safe and accepted.

As a teenager, I was bullied for my weight. It made me feel my body was not my own and in turn, I had very little self-worth. I can recall the heavy feeling of sadness, feeling tortured, feeling ugly, feeling not good enough. To compensate I focused on achieving high marks in school. However, being a great student cannot take away the shame and pain. By the time I was a senior in high school my strive for perfection and acceptance led me to an eating disorder. Bulimia and anorexia plagued me for years until I learned the coping skills necessary to recover from such a disorder. To look at food as fuel versus comfort and to embrace nourishing all areas of health—mind, body, and soul.

After high school, I declined scholarship opportunities and like most Greek diner kids jumped in to learn the family business. By nineteen I was running the overnight shift, making friends in the city, and partying as hard as I worked. Like a lightning bolt I was struck by wild young love at twenty-two-years-old. A love fueled by alcohol, drugs, and motorcycles in the rain. We eloped in Las Vegas. It didn't take long for things to quickly unravel and spiral out of control. I was completely addicted to drugs and my world was a dark place of dishonesty. My addiction had taken my spirit, and to survive it was fed by manipulation and lies. I was at the bottom of a downward spiral and life was completely unmanageable. There was a point at which things became volatile. This is when I made the decision to leave. A decision that was not mutual or well-received. I found myself choked unconscious, stomped, beaten, tied up, and tortured, staring down the barrel of a pistol. "Shhhhh. He whispered. You are going to die tonight. Don't cry." He caressed my face with the gun, while I sat there trying to untie my hands. I listened to him tell me where he was going to dump my body and how he intended to shoot both of my brothers. As he loaded the bullets into the gun, with all of the might in my heart, I prayed to God to send me an angel. At that very moment, the rope binding my wrists loosened. Truly miraculous, for I had been struggling to get free for hours. I ran out of the house into the street frantically screaming for help. My chest pumped with fear and urgency. "Faster feet, faster," I thought. Suddenly I felt my hair yanked and my knees crumbled beneath me. He had caught me. Instantly my hope deflated and he was dragging me down the street. "This time, you are not coming back out," he mumbled. It was then, a light from heaven, a divine intervention, an angel in disguise, my neighbor heard my screams. He got me to safety until the authorities arrived. Looking back today, I can see all of the ways God had protected me that night: freeing my hands, my neighbor waking up, I was barely injured despite being beaten for hours. It was as though I was shielded by the angels themselves.

Filled with shame and guilt from my situation and addiction, I did not have the courage to turn to my family for help. I found myself essentially homeless, broken, living like a nomad in my Jeep with a few boxes of belongings, a journal, LED Zeppelin II on cassette tape, and my kitten, Femmy. During the day, I would drive between several parking lots, sit a few hours, and relocate so as to not get noticed. I remember having less than $100 and knowing I had to make that last. My mind was constantly running trying to budget gas and food. I survived on an apple and a can of sardines everyday which I shared with my kitten. In the dark of the night, I would cry and let Jimmy Page and Robert Plant carry me away with the power of their music. My addiction led me to a painful reality, lonely and lost, not knowing where my next meal or shower would come from.

Somehow, despite the situation, I felt a bubble of love. A feeling of ultimate surrender. A feeling of survival, like a warrior. I knew I was meant for a different life, not the abyss I had been existing in, but a life of sharing light. Instead of pursuing drugs, I pursued God. That month in my car, I began my first gratitude journal, finding things on a daily basis to thank God for. To find hope. With no path present, I found myself praying often and trying to discover who exactly Eleni was. Eventually, I turned to my family and set a course of rebuilding a new life. Taking these steps also meant taking a journey of complete sobriety and eliminating alcohol. I quickly realized any substance that altered my mood only led me to danger. I am certainly not a first-time winner at trying. I just never gave up and kept working with the people my higher power sent to help me along the path of sobriety.

Looking back through my addictive history with food, substance abuse, and alcohol it was suddenly so clear. These addictions were what I was using to fill a void in my soul. A void fueled by a thousand forms of fear. The only way to combat fear is with faith ... all in, non-wavering faith. I had found salvation in the fellowship of people whose struggles were the same as mine. Through their selflessness and love, I finally felt whole. I learned to forgive, to look with an open, honest heart, accept my accountability, and address those I had caused harm. Most importantly, I learned that to maintain sobriety and connection with God, I had to give it away and help the still sick and suffering. Once I surrendered completely and focused on how I could best serve others, it is miraculous how quickly my life began picking up momentum.

Over the next few years I regained stability and took action toward a new career path in the health and wellness industry. I became a certified massage therapist, Reiki practitioner, nutritionist, and personal trainer. I went from feeling like a worthless human being, something you would scrape from the bottom of your shoe, to someone of value. Suddenly life was blooming and worth living.

Although I didn't have much in the way of material abundance, I was truly happy and fulfilled. There was not much money for food, but I would often come home to bushels of fresh produce on my door step from local farmers.

I felt gratitude and appreciation for the love and help I received from others. I found joy in things that cost nothing, such as fitness and empowering others with it, building a spiritual foundation with a higher power, Reiki, and service. I began focusing my energy by posting daily on social media seeking out those who were in dark places or struggling with their health. Each day I took those responses, ran five miles to the lake, meditated, and sent the healing energy of Reiki. It gave me a sense purpose and the feeling of reciprocating all of the love and blessings I had graciously received.

Through this period of transition, long-time family friends extended their hands of help to me and this is when I found my first mentor, Ray Rastelli Jr. He saw the light in me, and I soon found myself as the Health and Wellness Advisor for a division of his successful food corporation. I was given a company car and suddenly new opportunities and responsibilities seemed to be emerging on a daily basis. One of my roles was to train local celebrity, Tony Luke Jr.

Working side by side with Tony, I found his determination to hit his goals inspiring. His fight to succeed was relentless. He became the father figure in my life, sharing his wisdom with me. He encouraged me to keep climbing to the top, to focus on being in service, and to eliminate negative people from my circle. Ultimately, Tony lost over 100 pounds, and suddenly my name was in the papers and discussions on television and radio. With his successful weight loss came more blessings and my popularity as a trainer skyrocketed. I had found a true passion in motivating people to achieve their best overall health. My energy for it was unstoppable and so my peers accordingly gave me the nickname ELNRG.

Around the same time my position at RastelliFoods connected me with an incredible woman, author, and Complete Body Labs creator, Lydia Martinez Ebling. Our stories carried many of the same rock bottom struggles. She inspired me to shatter self-limiting beliefs and helped me focus on gratitude-based thinking and releasing past struggles. I was given the assignment to create healthy lifestyle programs and recipes to coincide with her already successful weight loss program. This also included traveling all over the country to speak and educate people about the connection between their food choices and health. Suddenly I was a corporate jet setter. Airplanes, PowerPoint presentations, big stages with bright lights. YES! I felt like I had finally arrived! Now, I realize thousands of people do this on a daily basis, but for this small-town Jersey girl, this was exhilarating. The excitement didn't stop, we filmed cooking segments in The Rastelli Foods Kitchen, shared the stage in front of thousands of people and pursued our similar passion to help people live their best lives. At this point in my life I felt validation for having courage and for not giving up, trusting fully all of the twists and turns my path had taken. It was surreal that less than three years prior I was broken, addicted, and existing in the dark. The girl who was trudging in the gutters had clawed her way out.

Corporate life would offer many exciting ventures including opening locations for Tony Luke as a culture trainer for general managers and employees all over the country. Most of all it offered me guidance from several strong individuals who saw the potential in me.

Life progressed and my dreams shifted when what seemed to be my fairy tale love arrived. In the midst of finding this joy, I experienced a shocking blow to my existence—a phone call at 5 o'clock in the morning that no one ever expects to get. My mother, my best friend, had taken her own life. I had spoken to her just two days prior and she was her upbeat, vivacious self. Her death was highly publicized and baffling to any who knew her. She was the laugh that shook a room. The smile that lit a dark day. My mother was personality personified. Forced to grieve in the public eye, I turned to the only way I knew to overcome pain: helping others. Friends came together to help me start fundraising for local animal organizations in her honor. We held events, increased awareness for suicide prevention, and helped local shelters. At the time it was difficult to understand her decision, however today I have come to accept my mother's life choices and see it as her way of taking her power back in a very powerless situation. In my heart I know I did all that I personally could do. Self-will always prevails, despite your most valiant efforts.

Where there is darkness, there is always light. Joyous news arrived. Six months later, I was pregnant! I would now take on life's most important role, motherhood. During my pregnancy, I made the decision to become a domestic violence volunteer responder. I knew the fear, I knew the pain, and what I knew most was that I could use my experience to be of service. I underwent extensive training to meet with abused women in their darkest hours at police stations and hospitals, offer comfort, guidance, and inform them of their options to live a healthy, safe life. My daughter, Zoe, was born healthy and happy. She was a much-needed blessing for my family. As time went on, the once charmed life changed, and it became clear my daughter's father and I had very different expectations. I didn't see motherhood as a reason to stop achieving. There was a fire burning in me, a calling not yet fulfilled, and I was not willing to give up on finding it. I knew in my heart if I continued on this path my passion would be extinguished and my voice would be silenced.

I made the difficult and bold decision to leave my relationship and take on life as a single mother. Eyes focused forward, it's humbling to see the miracles unfolding and my life rapidly picking up momentum. An earth angel, Kate Butler, kept appearing randomly in my life over the past three years. Her message of empowerment was strong, and it resonated with the same voice in my heart that told me to take this leap of faith and find my calling. When I was presented with an opportunity to write in her book series, I jumped all in. Connected to a strong core group of women, I am at a place in my life where I feel unstoppable. I know my purpose is to share my message of positive thinking and gratitude. I will use the pain of my past to inspire others. No matter the struggle, there is always a light of hope. The once beaten, addicted, abused woman who lived in fear is now standing in her power. Fueled by gratitude, faith and determination, my story defines me for a greater mission.

And I'm still standing.

ABOUT ELENI YIAMBILIS

Eleni Yiambilis, founder of EL-NRG.com is a motivational public speaker and certified Life and Thought Process Coach who found her calling in empowering individuals to shatter self-limiting beliefs and behaviors. Through ELNRG she helps people retrain the brain using her system appropriately named "The Gratitude Adjustment". Eleni has spoken across the country as an advocate for nutrition and fitness as a Health and Wellness Advisor for the Rastelli Foods Group.

Through fine-tuning the thought process from fear-based to faith-based, she has developed programs to assist others to achieve the same freedom. With over ten years' experience as a Reiki practitioner and crystal healer, she believes and teaches others how to attract their most vibrant, fulfilling life.

Eleni resides in southern New Jersey and is blessed with a spectacular daughter. She is a volunteer at a local women's and children's shelter where she responds to calls and counsels domestic violence victims. She also offers Reiki and life coaching to victims and assists the shelter in fundraising. Eleni has a true passion for fitness and enjoys utilizing the outdoors to help others feel healthy and inspired. Creative by nature, she enjoys upcycling antiques, woodworking, and any artistic venture. Her favorite place to be is by any natural body of water or cuddled up with her daughter.

Find her on the web at Elnrg.com
Facebook and Instagram Elnrg

*Log into Elnrg.com/illumination-special for a FREE gift!

REPRINTED WITH PERMISSIONS

Dr. Angela Williamson
Kate Butler
Gina Fresquez
Jennifer Granger
Jaaz Jones
Lisa Pezik
Samantha Ruth
Amy Broccoli
Victoria Chadderton
Liz Dowsett
Michelle Eades
Brenda Everts
Claudia Fernandez-Niedzielski
Angela Germano
Blair Hayse
Chloe Helms
Penelope Jones
Janice Lichtenwaldt
Fran Matteini
Cheryl McBride
Molly Peebles
Tina Raffa-Walterscheid
Chrisa Riviello
Virginia Rose
Mandy Scanlon
Alicia Thorp
Gina Walton
Katie Wood
Sondra Wyckoff
Eleni Yiambilis

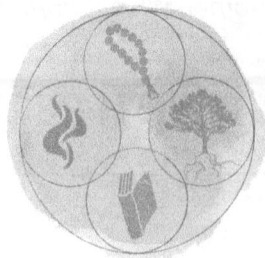

Are you a woman who inspires?
Are you a woman who impacts?
Are you a woman who illuminates the world?
Are you a woman who is ready to rise up?
Then we want to connect with you!

The *Inspired Impact Book Series* is looking to connect with women who desire to share their stories to inspire others and create a positive ripple effect in the world. If you have dreamed of publishing a book, then this is for you. If you have dreamed of bringing your message to a larger audience, then this is for you. If you have dreamed of expanding your business through a new platform, then this is for you. If you have dreamed of inspiring women all over the globe, then this is definitely for you!

We want to hear your story!

Visit www.katebutlerbooks.com to learn more about becoming a Featured Author in the #1 International Best-selling *Inspired Impact Book Series.*

May your soul be illuminated and your light shine brightly,

the women who illuminate

www.ingramcontent.com/pod-product-compliance
Lightning Source LLC
LaVergne TN
LVHW051226080426
835513LV00016B/1432